Charitable Choices

Charitable Choices

Philanthropic Decisions of Donors in the American Jewish Community

ARNOLD DASHEFSKY
AND
BERNARD LAZERWITZ

LEXINGTON BOOKS

A division of
ROWMAN & LITTLEFIELD PUBLISHERS, INC.
Lanham • Boulder • New York • Toronto • Plymouth, UK

LEXINGTON BOOKS

A division of Rowman & Littlefield Publishers, Inc.
A wholly owned subsidiary of The Rowman & Littlefield Publishing Group, Inc.
4501 Forbes Boulevard, Suite 200
Lanham, MD 20706

Estover Road
Plymouth PL6 7PY
United Kingdom

British Library Cataloguing in Publication Information Available

Library of Congress Cataloging-in-Publication Data

Dashefsky, Arnold.
  Charitable choices : philanthropic decisions of donors in the American Jewish
community / Arnold Dashefsky and Bernard Lazerwitz.
      p. cm.
  Includes bibliographical references and index.
  ISBN-13: 978-0-7391-0987-8 (hardcover : alk. paper)
  ISBN-10: 0-7391-0987-1 (electronic : alk. paper)
  ISBN-13: 978-0-7391-3250-0 (hardcover : alk. paper)
  ISBN-10: 0-7391-3250-4 (electronic : alk. paper)
  1. Charities—United States. 2. Welfare economics. 3. Jews—United States. I.
Lazerwitz, Bernard Melvin, 1926- II. Title.
  HV41.D37 2009
  361.7089'924073—dc22   2008043802

Printed in the United States of America

♾™ The paper used in this publication meets the minimum requirements of American
National Standard for Information Sciences—Permanence of Paper for Printed Library
Materials, ANSI/NISO Z39.48–1992.

Dedication

Dedicated to our Grandchildren, with the hope that they will pursue justice, aid in the repair of the world, and carry out deeds of loving kindness.

Contents

Preface

It should come as no surprise to readers of this volume that charitable giving and philanthropic behavior are frequently the subject of periodic media reports and newspaper headlines. Witness the following: "What Makes People Give?" (Leonhardt 2008), "Billionaire Gives a Big Gift but Still Gets to Invest It" (Strom 2006:A12), or "Charitable Giving Outpaces that from Other Disasters" (Strom: 2005:A24). It is no wonder that such stories are newsworthy when the giving of charity in 2005 exceeded one-quarter of a trillion dollars in the United States (AAFRC 2006:ii). This sum represented more than 2 percent of the gross domestic product (GDP) and that was a substantial increase over the first figure reported in 1954 of 1.5 percent of GDP (AAFRC 2005:11).

The above observation testifies to the significance of the phenomenon of charitable giving and philanthropic behavior as a topic for social scientific investigations. *The theme of this book is to understand and explain the motivations of individuals (including both incentives and barriers) to make charitable gifts as seen from the perspective of the donors and largely validated by the observations of directors of fundraising.* The topic becomes all the more important in recent years as politicians have tried to deflect government assumed responsibilities for charity and welfare and direct them to private agencies and religious institutions. Indeed, "charitable choice," as commonly described in the contemporary period, refers to "a set of rules that encourage 'faith-based organizations' (FBOs) to participate in government-funded welfare programs" (Hoover 2001:183). Walsh (2001:1) has suggested that the term was introduced into the political arena in 1996 by former United States Senator John Ashcroft. This effort is a dramatic reversal of a trend of growing government assumption of such responsibilities since the collapse of European feudalism led to the creation of the urban poor.

Our focus, however, is on "charitable choices," an examination of motivations for charitable giving. This topic might best be achieved through an examination of both quantitative and qualitative data on which this volume relies. In order to amass the array of data, the current investigation limited itself to one religio-ethnic community, American Jews, for which there were several data sources and a generally acknowledged and popular perception for philanthropic generosity. We have benefited from following this line of research for more than two decades and we draw on data sources spanning more than three decades, including quantitative data from the National Jewish Population Surveys of 1971, 1990, and 2000-01, supplemented by qualitative data gathered with a variety of donors and non-donors in the 1980s and amplified by interviews with professional fundraisers carried out after the turn of the millennium. The latter findings largely supported the qualitative data produced in the 1980s.

Chapter One presents an overview of the evolution of charitable donations and philanthropy in the social scientific analysis of gift-giving and the alternative approaches for studying it. Chapter Two documents such giving in the Jewish community, offering contrasts to the approach of Christianity, and concludes with an overview of data and methods utilized in this study. Chapter Three provides quantitative evidence from three National Jewish Population Surveys on the sources of philanthropic giving.

The next three chapters highlight the findings from a qualitative study of three categories of individuals in the Jewish community: "*Donors*" or good givers to the central Jewish fundraising campaign; "*Unaffiliated*" or those who generally don't give and don't formally belong to a Jewish organization or synagogue; and an intermediate group of the "*Affiliated*" who belong to a Jewish organization or synagogue but did not give to the central fundraising campaign. Chapter Four describes the differences of the three groups in their Jewish and general social and economic characteristics and highlights the similarities to the national sample described in Chapter Three. Chapter Five examines in greater detail the orientation to charitable giving of the three groups, first presented in Chapter Four. Chapter Six details the incentives and barriers to such giving among the three groups described in the previous chapters.

The last chapter to report data, Chapter Seven, offers recent qualitative findings from a set of interviews with professional fundraisers in order to assess the usefulness of the data gathered previously from the individual donors and non-donors reported in the preceding chapter. Finally, Chapter Eight offers a brief summary of the findings and includes both practical as well as theoretical implications for fundraising. Most notably, we conclude, based on our research and that of others, that charitable giving is facilitated among those who identify with the norms of the community and are enmeshed in a communal network.

There is a parable recounted by Kimmelman which refers to the Land of Israel:

The Jordan River streams down the eastern border of the Land of Israel connecting the Kinneret, or Sea of Galilee, with the Dead Sea, or Salt Sea. Since both seas are fed by the same Jordan River, what makes the Kinneret so sweet and life-giving and the Dead Sea so salty and destructive to life? The Kinneret not only receives, but also gives of its waters while the Dead Sea keeps all it receives—thus its name. To paraphrase Scripture (Proverbs 10:2), "Helping others keeps you alive." Or, as some would say, "People who are needed by people are the happiest people of all" (1982:21).

If it is true that sustaining life requires both the acts of receiving from and giving to others, then the way to create a life-giving community and a flourishing society is to encourage both private philanthropy and public responsibility for providing for the needs of all citizens. Support for such a goal is to affirm the toast: "To Life!"

Acknowledgments

Over the course of more than two decades of investigation of the topic of charitable giving and philanthropic behavior, we have benefited from the advice and assistance of many individuals. Our research effort began with the study of seventy-two donors and potential donors to the former United Jewish Appeal (UJA), which was conducted in the 1980s, and funded by the UJA, under the professional leadership of Miriam Cantor and Barry Gradman, and supported by their lay chair, Neil Cooper. We offer our thanks to them and to their colleagues, Neal Hurwitz and Barry Judelman.

Our research expanded from a qualitative study to a quantitative examination of data from several National Jewish Population Surveys. In both phases, a number of colleagues in the social sciences offered valuable advice and assistance in the development of our empirical investigation and preparation of this book. We would like to express our appreciation to them, including Mark Abrahamson, Mark Chaves, Hsu-Chih Cheng, Steven M. Cohen, Egon Mayer (z"l), Paul Schervish, Jim Schwartz, and Jerry Winter. In addition, we also would like to acknowledge the encouragement we derived from the research on charitable giving conducted by our colleagues, Barry Chiswick, William V. D'Antonio, Daniel Elazar (z"l), Virginia Hodgkinson, Dean Hoge, Teresa Odendahl, Francie Ostrower, Gary Tobin, and Jack Wertheimer, as well as the many other scholars and authors whom we cited.

One of the benefits of conducting research at a university is the opportunity to interact with students and to draw on their contributions as research assistants. We would like to thank several undergraduate and graduate students at the University of Connecticut, who provided assistance, from both the Department of Sociology and the Center for Judaic Studies and Contemporary Jewish Life. Undergraduates included Celeste Machado, Rachelle Rosenberg, and David Zeligson; and graduate students working at the Center included Ilana Cone, Laura Gottfried, Jessica Hartke, Mira Levine, Katherine Peveler, and Rebekah Shapiro. Special thanks are also extended to graduate students Dinur Blum, Amanda Edwards, and Marilyn Rothstein for their careful proofreading of the manuscript and to Dustin Stein for his faithful coding of data for Chapter Seven. In addition, Sam Richardson, graduate assistant in Sociology and at the North

American Jewish Data Bank at UConn, provided very valuable help. Finally, we would like to acknowledge the bibliographic assistance of Dana L. Kline in the first phase of the research.

Throughout our research effort, and especially in the final phase of interviews with experts in the field of Jewish federation fundraising, we were aided by the many insights we derived from the following communal professionals: Stephen Abramson, Daniel R. Allen, David Altshuler, Robert P. Aronson, Phyllis Cook, Ted Farber, Michael D. Fischer, John R. Fishel, Joel Fox, Darrell D. Friedman, Irv Geffen, Jeffrey Klein, Max L. Kleinman, H. Jack Mayer, Harry Nadler, Ami Nahshon, Steve Nasatir, Steve Rakitt, Barry Rosenberg, Gary Rubin, Jon Ruskay, Edith Samers, Barry Shrage, Stephen D. Solender, and Jacob Solomon. In addition, the following professionals also were very helpful in assisting in launching the research effort: Ed Alcosser, Don Cooper, Suzanne Jacobson, and Mark Silverman. We likewise wish to acknowledge the contribution of two other professionals in the field, Lorraine Blass and Bob Evans, who read parts of the manuscript and offered helpful comments.

Indebted as we are, we would also like to acknowledge the administrative and technical assistance we received from staff members of the Center for Judaic Studies and Contemporary Jewish Life at the University of Connecticut, including Linda Snyder (z"l) and Dianne Tillman, as well as undergraduate assistants, Ariel Borgendale, Jennifer Rubino, and Emily Sullivan. Special thanks are extended to Lorri Lafontaine, who prepared the camera-ready copy of the manuscript in her ever-gracious and cheerful manner. To all of those we named, we extend our sincere thanks and to any others we may have inadvertently omitted, we offer our profound apologies.

We would also like to express our appreciation to our academic homes, the University of Connecticut, which provided grant funding through its Research Foundation and sabbatic as well as research leave to facilitate the preparation of this book and to Bar-Ilan University for its unlimited computer support. This support permitted the complex and time consuming use of the complicated statistical computer systems needed for a thorough study of the National Jewish Population Surveys.

In this connection, we would also like to offer thanks to the Mandell L. Berman Institute—North American Jewish Data Bank, chaired by Mandell L. (Bill) Berman, its board and staff, currently located at the University of Connecticut, for creating an enduring legacy of available data for posterity, on which we continue to draw. In this effort at the Data Bank, we are aided by associate director, Ron Miller, and assistant director, Cory Lebson, as well as the staff of the United Jewish Communities, including Lou Feldstein, Laurence

Kotler-Berkowitz and Jonathan Ament, and we express our thanks to them for their encouragement. Penultimately, we want to express our appreciation to our editors at Lexington Books, Jessica Bradfield, Julie Kirsch, Alex Masulis, Joseph Parry, and Ryan Quick, whose patience and encouragement are greatly appreciated, and to two anonymous reviewers who offered many helpful suggestions.

Lastly, we offer special thanks to all of the people who consented to be interviewed. Without them, there would be no book and we would have nothing to say. It is our hope that our collective effort will not only provide illumination on the topic of charitable choices but also enlightenment in the development of sound policies to advance the well-being of all members of the community and the larger society.

Chapter One

Why People Give Charity:
A Philanthropic Phenomenon Based on
Consumer Spending, Situation,
Self-Interest, or Socialization?

"Can America serve as a democratic society if everyone has rights and no one has responsibilities?" asked an advertisement for a public-policy journal. The publication, founded by a group of scholars, seeks to probe the balance or imbalance between the rights of individuals and the needs of the community. One intellectual area of inquiry where the dilemma between rights and responsibilities emerges is the social arena of charity. How people choose to help one another reveals a great deal about the cohesiveness and social solidarity of any particular social system or group.

Contemporary politicians over the last two decades have argued that the United States exhibits that social cohesiveness. The first president of the twenty-first century, George W. Bush, a Republican, sought to cultivate "faith-based charity" as a solution to social problems. His father, former President George Bush, spoke of a "thousand points of light" in the 1980s and implied in his campaign that Americans would feel sufficient obligation to both one another and the society at large to contribute time and money toward the common good. Nor is this approach confined to one party, as evidenced by the Democratic President Bill Clinton's signing of a bill in the 1990s to end "welfare as we know it" (where welfare represents governmental charity). Instead, it was expected that the charitable inclinations of American business and civic groups, as well as individuals, would step in to offer jobs to those formerly on welfare.

Thus in the recent past, there emerged a bipartisan effort to shift the government's responsibility to the charitable whims of the citizenry. This book examines the charitable behavior of individuals and the incentives and barriers to such activity. It is hoped, therefore, that the findings may contribute to a dispassionate assessment of the optimal balance between public and private philanthropy.

1

Evolution of Charitable Donations and Philanthropy as Gifts

When one makes a charitable donation, does one expect anything in return? It is a gift, or "something that is bestowed voluntarily and without compensation," as a college dictionary defined it. Nevertheless, as social anthropologists have pointed out, the gift "is most often used with reference to the exchange of goods and services which, although regarded as voluntary by the people involved, is in all societies part of the behavior expected of persons in specific social relationships. Such 'gifts' . . . are normally given with a clear expectation that some return will be made . . ." (Stirling 1964:289). The most celebrated early exponent of this approach was Mauss (1954/1925), who examined how the exchange of gifts served a useful social function in producing cohesion and solidarity in a community or society. (For a fuller discussion of *The Gift Economy* and its relationship to the moral order, see Cheal 1988.)

Therefore, it is most helpful to view charitable donations or philanthropic behavior as a form of gift-giving. How may we distinguish between the terms "philanthropy" and "charity?" They have often been used interchangeably, but changes in attitude to the phenomenon of giving have meant that charity now has a somewhat derogatory connotation and is gradually giving way to the more acceptable concept of philanthropy (Ross 1968:72). It is defined in a standard college dictionary as "the effort or inclination to increase the well-being of [hu]mankind, as by charitable aid or donations." In point of fact, however, philanthropy may be viewed popularly as the "money given" and the philanthropist as the "wealthy person who makes gifts" (Hoge and Griffin 1992:5). Philanthropy literally means love of humankind whereas charity is defined in the same dictionary as "the provision of help or relief to the poor; almsgiving." In this book, we will use both terms as they are popularly conceived of as synonymous even though the gifts of philanthropists may have more to do with supporting their own lifestyle (i.e., funding a museum) than redistributing wealth to the poor (i.e., donating to a soup kitchen). This conforms to the distinction introduced by Ostrower: "Charity is specifically directed toward the poor, and often focuses on the relief of severe and immediate needs. Philanthropy is a broader concept, which includes charity but also encompasses the wider range of private giving for public purposes" (1995:4).

In the ancient world, charity grew out of religious systems as in Egypt, ancient Israel, and later Christianity. The notion of the tithe derives from the *Tanakh* or Hebrew Bible, which required the giving of one-tenth (*maaser*) of one's income for charity, a practice adopted by the Church of Christ of Latter Day Saints, the Mormons. An excellent historical review of philanthropy by Ross (1968) showed that such a notion was also present in Islamic, Confucian, and Hindu thought. While charity had its roots in religious traditions, "the great changes that took place in the whole conception and organization of charity were due, first of all, to the decline of medieval society in Europe and to the ensuing disorganization which loosed forces that gradually undermined the former, tightly structured, feudal way of life" (Ross 1968:74). This decline led to a movement from rural to urban areas and growing poverty, exacerbated by wars and plagues. Poverty became a more serious social problem and the church, which formerly had organized charity, needed private and secular charities to help address the issue. "Thus historical circumstances, which shifted the power of the former feudal lords and the medieval church, redistributed wealth and power, and brought about the beginning of a new industrial society, also caused a redistribution and responsibility for charity" (Ross 1968:74). Soon philanthropy was supported in the law passed by Queen Elizabeth I in England in 1601, which required the local community to look after the poor. *Thus philanthropy was now no longer a religious responsibility alone but also a secular public and private obligation.* As modernization gradually took hold, the state came to assume more and more of a responsibility for the welfare of the population. Countries in Scandinavia, England, and the British Commonwealth states were among the first to create the "social welfare" state (Ross 1968).

While the United States was slower to adopt the principle of the welfare state, "the expansion of philanthropy and its new form of organization have gone further . . . in the United States, than in any other part of the world" (Ross 1968:76). Some would say that the twentieth century witnessed a "philanthropic revolution." Nevertheless, the skeptical attitude towards government control and reliance on individualism helped to shape the character of private philanthropy in the United States. The business community viewed the provision of charitable gifts as a means to maintain control over segments of society without government intervention. Moreover, poverty was seen as the fault of the poor for lacking initiative and being apathetic.

Even in America, however, there emerged the recognition that rapid urbanization and industrialization could not be dealt with by private charity alone, especially after the Great Depression of the 1930s. As the government assumed more of a role in social welfare, subsequent post-World War Two affluence led to substantial increases in private donations—both by corporations and individuals (Ross 1968). *Thus by the twentieth century, philanthropy, which was seen in the ancient world as a religious obligation, was well integrated into both the public and private sectors. Efforts by some politicians to restore charity to its faith-based roots may be viewed by some as reactionary and a return to the premodern origins of philanthropy, notwithstanding the important and useful connection between religion and philanthropy. While in some societies religion receives state support, the wall of separation in the United States keeps the two sectors apart. Therefore, it is unlikely that religious institutions alone can afford to serve the needs of the poor.*

Philanthropy and Religion

The issue of charitable giving is all the more socially significant in that billions of dollars of such donations are made each year and more traditional religious group members are very generous to their churches (see Stark and Finke 2000). "Ranging from charity to sacrifice, and entailing the cultivation of such related virtues as love, kindness, generosity or compassion, gift-giving is clearly a tenet of central importance in all the 'great,' 'other worldly' religions" (Silber 2000:115). This observation seems to be supported empirically by data reported in *Giving USA 2006* (AAFRC 2006), wherein the single greatest beneficiaries of American philanthropy (although not the majority of funds contributed) were religious congregations (36 percent of all contributions). This large sum of money is raised through a variety of methods. According to Hoge and Griffin, religious giving is carried out in five ways: 1) annual pledge drives, 2) special annual appeals, 3) capital fund campaigns, 4) additional appeals for educational, health and welfare causes, and 5) fees for services (1992:21–22).

The $93.18 billion in religious giving in 2005 was 5.9 percent higher than in 2000 (2.5 percent after accounting for inflation). The plurality of philanthropic funds devoted to religion may not be so surprising given the fact that Weitzman *et al.* (2002) reported 353,606 houses of worship in the United States for Christians, Jews and Muslims and also 11,416 religious organizations which filed IRS Form 990 in 1998 (cited in AAFRC 2002:98).

How widespread is religious affiliation and attendant charitable giving? Again, the annual benchmark reference, *Giving USA 2002* (AAFRC 2002), summarizing research carried out on this topic in 2000 reported that 88 percent of Americans in a national sample said they had some religious affiliation, 58 percent belonged to a specific house of worship or religious organization, 45 percent attended religious activities at least weekly and 70 percent contributed to religion. Two other studies found that the average gift per individual was $886 and per donating household was $1,620 (with average household size at 2.59 in 2000).

Hoge et al. examined personal giving within five American Christian religious groups, Assemblies of God, Baptists, Catholics, Lutherans, and Presbyterians; and, based on this set of churches, noted five basic facts about philanthropic giving and church giving in the United States:

1. The majority of all philanthropic giving in the United States goes to churches. . . .
2. The increase in religious giving over a recent twenty-five year period was somewhat lower than the rate of inflation. . . .
3. The level of giving to churches varies greatly, depending on the denomination. . . .

4. The amounts given by church members in any congregation vary wide-
    ly. . . .
5. Trends in giving result in a long-term decline in funds available to the
    national denominations for their programs and compel a downsizing of
    programs and staff (1996:11–15).

For more on financing American religion, see Chaves and Miller (2002).

An earlier nationwide study on religious giving by Hodgkinson and Weitzman (1986) found that those who were more involved in their religious congregations were more likely to contribute more generously to religious charities.
They further reported that 75 percent of Protestants gave to religious charities
and slightly fewer Catholics (71 percent) did so. They concluded that "the survey results did not show a clear relationship between giving to religion and giving to other charities. What it did show was that those who were very involved
in their church or synagogue gave more generously to religious charities"
(1986:41).

Similarly, a Canadian study found that 51 percent of Protestants and 49 percent of Catholics made religious donations. As in the findings in the United
States, a correlation between religiosity and religious giving was uncovered
(Mollenhauer 1987); but a national British survey of charitable behavior, for
example, failed to examine religious differences at all (Saxon-Harrold and Carter 1987).[1]

Greeley and McManus (1987) earlier had sought to understand why Catholics contributed less than Protestants to their respective churches. They found
that Catholics, in comparison to Protestants, were not inherently less generous,
did not earn less, gave similarly when controlling for family size and tuition
costs, and were no less committed to their religion. One finding, however, did
stand out. While Protestants and Catholics who were less religiously observant
were similar in their charitable behavior, Protestants who attended church regularly and considered religion important were much more generous than Catholics. It appears that an important factor in explaining this difference was the
greater alienation of Catholics from the moral teachings of the Church, such as
those dealing with contraception and abortion. This finding is supported by the
research of D'Antonio et al. (1989).

The connection between philanthropy and religion is also demonstrated by a
study of 4,216 American adults twenty-one and older, which reported the following:

> Givers and volunteers to religious congregations are more generous with their
> money and time than those not motivated to support religion. This conclusion
> crosses income categories remaining valid even when economic status is taken
> into account. The most generous are those households that both give and volun-
> teer to religious congregations, expressing their beliefs, values and commitment
> by contributing both money and time to causes that are important to them (In-

dependent Sector 2002:36).

Furthermore, the study found that religious givers contributed more generously than those who gave to secular causes and "they are at least as generous, if not more so, toward secular organizations than are people who give only to secular causes" (Independent Sector 2002:36).

Hoge (1994) laid out six assumptions, based on empirical research, about church giving:

1. Religious giving is rational behavior and can be modeled using existing sociological and economic methods. . . .
2. People strongly committed to God and God's promises will give more money to the church. . . .
3. Church members who have more discretionary income will, on average, give more to the church. . . .
4. The distribution of the amount of money given by members of any church is greatly skewed. . . .
5. The amount of money potentially available to churches from members is a variable sum, not a fixed sum (1994:102–103).

In a related work, Hoge and Griffin (1992) reviewed previous research and found that the following variables were positively associated with the level of religious contributions: income, education, having children, church attendance, use of pledge cards, Orthodox belief, and personal faith. In addition, they reported that age is positively associated with increased giving until about age sixty. Percentage of family income donated usually is related to income as is size of congregation. Finally, they report no strong relationship between quality of parish services or quantity of parish staff and church giving.[2]

Thus, the link between charity and religion in ancient civilization endures today in the greater philanthropic generosity of givers to religious congregations. They may be distinguished from secular givers who contribute to other charities, e.g., health and educational organizations but not to religious congregations. Of course, many individuals give both to religious congregations (including churches, synagogues, temples and mosques (but not schools, hospitals, etc. connected to a religious body) as well as secular organizations devoted to health, education and the like, which may be associated with a religious group (for example, Catholic Charities or the United Jewish Communities).

Dimensions of Philanthropy in the United States

While religion may be an incentive for charitable giving, our interest is in understanding and explaining such behavior in general and not just in religious giving. Therefore, we may ask how large is the enterprise of philanthropy in the United

States? Figure 1.1 presents the rise in giving over a forty-year period. According to *Giving USA 2002* (AAFRC 2002), total charitable giving was $212 billion in 2001 (including contributions following the attacks on September 11, 2001), which represented a 0.5 percent increase (-2.3 percent, adjusted for inflation) from the $211 billion in 2000. For 2004, the amount rose to $245 billion and for 2005 went up to $260 billion (including disaster relief for Hurricane Katrina), which equaled 2.1 percent of Gross Domestic Product, and it has been more than 2 percent since 1997 (AAFRC 2006:32).

The sources of this generosity in 2005 flow from four fountains of wealth according to *Giving USA 2006* (AAFRC 2006:14):

1. *Individuals*: $199.07 billion (76.5 percent);
2. *Bequests*: $17.44 billion (6.7 percent);
3. *Foundations (excluding Corporations)*: $30.0 billion (11.5 percent); and
4. *Corporations*: $13.77 billion (5.3 percent).

The above results are summarized in Figure 1.2.

Who benefits from such largesse? According to *Giving USA 2006* (AAFRC 2006:16), the main beneficiaries are the following causes in dollars contributed and percent of total gifts. The total was $260.25 billion in 2005.

1. *Religious Congregations and Denominations*: $93.18 billion (35.8 percent);
2. *Education*: $38.56 billion (14.8 percent);
3. *Human Services*: $25.36 billion (9.7 percent);
4. *Health*: $22.54 billion (8.7 percent);
5. *Public Society Benefit Organizations*: $14.03 billion (5.4 percent);
6. *Arts, Culture and Humanities*: $13.51 billion (5.2 percent);
7. *Environmental or Animal Causes*: $8.86 billion (3.4 percent);
8. *International Affairs*: $6.39 billion (2.5 percent);
9. *Foundations and Unallocated Giving*: $37.85 billion (14.5 percent).

The above results are summarized in Figure 1.3.

Figure 1.4 presents the changes in giving for a forty-year period by examining eight consecutive five-year spans from 1966–2005. Charitable giving in the 2001–05 period was 17.5 percent greater than in the period of 1996–2000, adjusting for inflation (AAFRC 2006:31). When the economy has grown, giving has increased faster than inflation. However, not surprisingly, when the economy is in recession, contributions fall in real dollars as they did by 2.3 percent in 2001. In recession years, giving in real dollars drops an average of 1.1 percent; and when there is no recession, contributions rise an average 3.8 percent in real dollars. While individual giving has increased in real dollars in each five-year period, the remaining sectors have had a more up-and-down experience in inflation-adjusted dollars (AAFRC 2002:22–23).

The giving of charity by individuals, which is the main theme of this book, is the major source of all donations as reported by Giving USA 2006. It is estimated that of all total contributions by individuals totaling $199.07 billion in 2005, this sum represented 2.8 percent of personal consumption expenditure, excluding food and energy (AAFRC 2006:39). In 1965, this proportion stood at 3.8 percent and gradually declined to 2.4 percent in 1995; but since then, it began to rise, peaking at 3.2 percent in 2000 and stabilizing at 2.8 percent in 2005 (AAFRC 2006:39). Perhaps individual citizens have responded to the political shift from public to private responsibility for charity as noted at the outset of this chapter.[3]

Figure 1.1 Total Giving, 1965-2005 ($ in Billions)

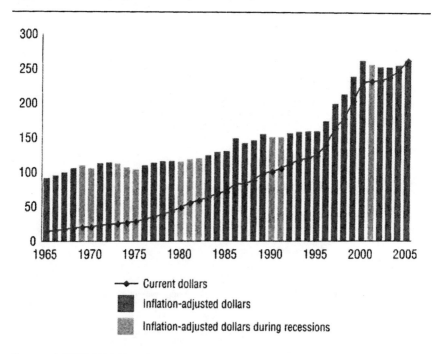

Source: AAFRC 2006:30 (Adapted and reprinted with permission)

Figure 1.2 2005 Contributions: $260.28 Billion by Source of Contributions

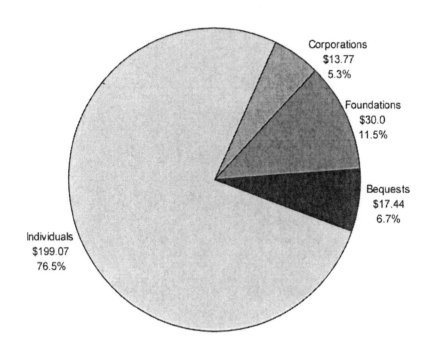

All figures are rounded. Total may not be 100%

Source: AAFRC 2006:14 (Adapted and reprinted with permission)

Figure 1.3 2005 Contributions: $260.28 Billion by Type of Recipient Organization

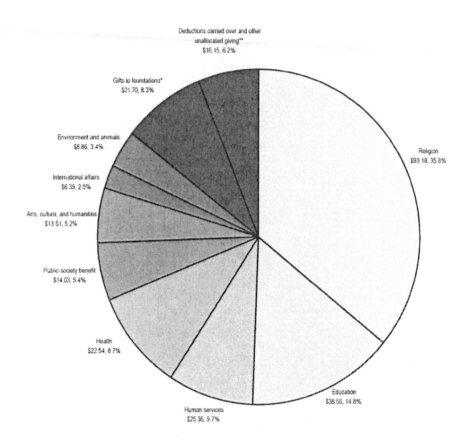

All figures are rounded. Total may not be 100%.
  *Foundation Center estimate.
**"This amount represents individual and corporate deductions expected to be claimed in 2005 for
  gifts made in prior years (carried over) . . ." (AAFRC 2006:17).

Source: AAFRC 2006:16 (Adapted and reprinted with permission)

Figure 1.4 Total Giving by Source by Five-Year Spans in Inflation-Adjusted Dollars, 1966–2005 ($ in Billions)

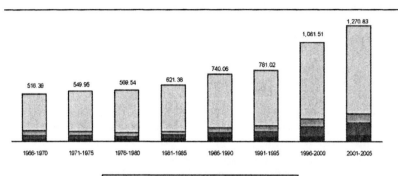

Period	Corporations	Foundations	Bequests	Individuals
1966-1970	23.69	43.84	46.43	402.43
1971-1975	21.82	41.90	49.36	436.87
1976-1980	25.46	32.15	35.30	476.63
1981-1985	35.32	36.37	42.09	507.60
1986-1990	43.50	51.06	53.24	592.26
1991-1995	43.12	62.24	64.27	611.39
1996-2000	54.15	104.18	93.20	829.98
2001-2005	61.70	147.17	100.38	961.59

Source: AAFRC 2006:31 (Adapted and reprinted with permission)

Can Charity Fill the Gap?
Alternative Approaches Accounting for Philanthropic Behavior

The political revolution in the past few decades of the devolution of responsibility (see Hall 1997) for the poor, the ill, and the infirm from the government to the citizenry makes the topic for this book all the more urgent and compelling. Recognizing this apparent late twentieth century trend, *Time* magazine asked in a lead story in the "Society" section, "Can Charity Fill the Gap?" (Van Biema 1995). In fact, the Presidents' Summit for America's Future convened in Philadelphia in 1997, with its laudatory objectives, highlighted this trend. More recently, Leonhardt (2008), in *The New York Times Magazine*, examined the question, "What Makes People Give?"[4] Both popular and scholarly interest in charitable giving appear to have increased as such philanthropy continues to grow to hundreds of billions of dollars although the literature still may be described as "thin."

Social scientific conceptualizations of charity, however, may question the expectations of American politicians for filling the gap created by the lessening of government responsibility. A variety of approaches exist in understanding philanthropic behavior among social scientists. They may be broadly classified as *economic, psychological* and *sociological/anthropological* although there may be some overlap among them.

In the *economic* realm, Chiswick (1991) succinctly summarized three different models to explain the apparent "uneconomic" behavior of philanthropy. The first approach, referred to as the "neoclassical" view, regards philanthropy as a consumer good. (Chiswick cited the work of Schwartz 1970, Feldstein and Taylor 1976 and Boskin and Feldstein 1977 as sources for this approach.) Thus, individuals seek "to maximize an unmeasurable item called 'utility' by consuming goods and services such as housing, food and movies. It is the finiteness of resources in terms of both money (and income) and time, that constrain or limit consumption" (Chiswick 1991:5). Therefore, philanthropy is regarded as another type of good. Thus,

> the reduction in tax rates in the 1980s [under President Reagan] had the perhaps unintended consequence of sharply reducing the incentives for philanthropic contributions. There was, therefore, an inherent inconsistency in the Reagan administration's joint objectives of expanding the volunteering sector and simultaneously reducing the federal government's taxes and expenditures on social services, the arts and related activities (Chiswick 1991:6).

Of course, the same could be said of the effect of President Bush's twenty-first-century tax cut.

Two other models are proposed by Chiswick as more compelling explanations and they are the "altruism" and "club" approaches:

> The altruism approach requires identification with the recipient and can be effective for understanding behavior with small close groups such as the family. The club model implies identification with other donors and is more compelling for understanding what is generally referred to as philanthropy (1991:12).

A useful empirical study, based on a random national sample of 2,432 households along with 359 high income tax payers explored the relationship between gifts of money and time. Ferris and Woolley (1991) found a significant correlation between volunteering and charitable contributions. The determinants of the latter were represented in an economic model taking into account income, effective price of giving (after-tax cost), age, wealth, number of children in the household, and religion.

The *psychological* approach emphasizes the situational circumstances surrounding charitable gifts. Individuals give because they find themselves in an immediate situation where they are constrained to do so. For example, the giver's perception of giving can be manipulated. Reece (1979) defined philanthropic behavior as involving the voluntary transfer of economic goods to an organization or individual. The donor makes the decision to give or not based on a whole range of preconceived attitudes and values which may be influenced by the way he or she is approached. The less an institution speaks of its own needs and the more it emphasizes the tangible or intangible benefits gotten from such contributions, the more successful the campaign. According to Lord (1981) the message to be projected by organized charitable institutions should emphasize the donor's opportunity to become part of a larger goal. For example, Lord discussed the situation of a theater in a large urban area, which held an annual drive to raise funds to cover its financial deficits. Instead of emphasizing its monetary problems, the appeal emphasized the fact that the donors by their contributions were making a commitment and an investment in their city. In addition, it is helpful in some ways to show why it is beneficial for the donor to make a contribution.

Other studies examined the role of the solicitation context. Benson and Catt (1978) in their study investigated whether attitudes and varied verbal requests for money in a door-to-door United Way campaign produced any significant differences in financial contributions. A twenty-eight-year-old female canvassed a lower- and middle-class neighborhood for three weeks during the same hours, Monday through Friday. Three variables tested were: 1) whether those to receive the charitable donation projected a high or low dependency, 2) whether the donor responded to a preconceived notion of social responsibility, or 3) whether the statement "it makes you feel good to give" prompted a donation. They concluded that the donor gave more when he or she felt those in need were in this situation due to some external cause such as environment, heredity, or disease. Verbal pleas referring to moral weakness, lack of motivation, or personal choice were not nearly as effective. When told that giving a contribution "will make you feel good," donors responded more readily than those who were told it was their social responsibility to contribute. The most productive approach was a verbal presentation, which included a reference to external needs and the "feel-good reason."

Reingen (1978) concluded in his research that when soliciting for a donation, the verbal presentation can influence the amount given. When donors were told, "As part of the fundraising drive, I'm collecting for the Heart Association," the compliance rate was 11 percent. However, when the solicitor added, "Even a penny will help," the compliance rate jumped to 39 percent. Do the donors somehow feel that even at the low rate, giving will accumulate and the sum will grow to be a substantial amount? Does "even a penny" allow the person to become part of a larger goal? While these questions were not addressed in the study, they require further examination.

Most literature that has addressed effective methods of solicitation stressed face-to-face contact rather than use of the phone or mail. Generally, it has been found important to make available facts about budget allocations, noting what percent actually goes to the program versus what is used for overhead.

Attitudes toward charitable giving were also affected by age and gender. Sundel (1978) reported findings from the responses of 267 persons who participated in a survey of attitudes toward the United Way. He tested the hypothesis that the application of methods used by profit-making businesses could be used also to increase donations from prospective donors. Sundel attempted to discover whether there existed a range of attitudes toward giving; and if so, whether this would indicate a need to segment the population, educating each group according to perceived values. Variables used were age, gender, management, and non-management employees of four different concerns. Sundel noted that managers were more in favor of a joint campaign as were older employees; therefore, the target group of education should be aimed at the younger employees who needed to be brought into the tradition of contributing a "fair share" to maintain social services.

Harris, Benson, and Hall (1975) studied the behavior of individuals observed leaving a Catholic church when requests for contributions to the March of Dimes were sought. Their hypothesis stated that confession served to reduce guilt and thus decrease subsequent altruism. Seventy-four adult men and ninety-nine adult women, alone or with others, were asked to give money, and the amounts were recorded. It was important to note that contributions by men were higher prior to confession while women donated larger amounts post-confessional. Both men and women gave more when with someone else and, overall, men donated more than women. It should be noted that this idea of men giving more than women may be tied to other issues. Men have traditionally earned more money and thus may feel more in control of dispensing charity dollars. This then is open to change as women move into higher ranks of the work force. Also, women have traditionally donated to charity in other ways, such as volunteering their time rather than money.

Benson and Catt (1978) also found that males gave more than females in their door-to-door United Way Campaign Study. They added that perhaps female generosity was linked to social expectations concerning appropriate role behavior. Women traditionally have been oriented to socio-emotional activities and hence "donated" time, attention, understanding, and solace; men traditionally have been more oriented toward instrumental activities and hence were responsible for allocating financial resources.

While a substantial portion, nevertheless, of the social science literature on charitable giving tends to be derived more from the psychological tradition, an excellent review of the *sociological* and *anthropological* literature, however, is provided by Galaskiewicz (1985). He presented a variety of such accounts on the role of gifts and gift-giving in society. Relying on a "nominalist" theoretical framework, he concluded that selective incentives provide the basis for sustaining such gifts. This theoretical orientation is rooted in the dominant Western conception that the motivation for particular individual behaviors is simply the maximization of personal self-interest. According to this approach, an ethic of communitarianism does not appear to play a role in the motivation for the giving of gifts of charity. Thus economic studies, focusing on consumer spending; psychologically oriented studies, drawing on situational factors; and sociologically and anthropologically oriented studies, emphasizing rational self-interest, fail to reveal a potentially more profound basis for charitable activity that may be rooted in the process of socialization to a set of norms, beliefs, and values favoring such acts.

Such a *social psychological* conception provides a somewhat different direction to the study of helping behavior and is based on a "normative approach." Berkowitz and Connor (1966) found experimental support for the "norm of social responsibility," i.e., the more people are dependent on others, the more they will receive help. Similarly, Gouldner (1960) defined the "norm of reciprocity" as based on the notion that the more people have been helped by others, the more help they should give in return. This approach is consistent with Ostrower's more recent research, which focused on the "normative basis of elite philanthropy" (1995). Ostrower interviewed ninety-nine elite individuals who gave major gifts of money to New York City non-profit organizations. Her study (response rate of 80 percent) "focuses on the meaning and sources of philanthropy as a social institution among the elite. . . . In the process, philanthropy comes to function as a mark of class status that is connected to elite identity" (1995:25). She reported that elites must change to survive and therefore she found that newly affluent individuals who were previously excluded (like the Jews) were included in the 1980s. Thus, elite philanthropic giving is tied to the development of "elite culture, identity and cohesion" (1995:27).

Ostrower further showed how elite philanthropy was integrated into the social and cultural life of this stratum in the population, which reflected their interest in culture and education. The donors' gender as well as religious and ethnic identities played a role in their charitable behavior. An exception to the trend, reported only anecdotally and not empirically, has to do with the technology-based wealth of California philanthropy, which emerged in the 1990s, and was noted by the president of the Community Foundation Silicon Valley, Peter Hero: "A lot of wealth has been made very quickly and there is an exuberance about giving which is done less in terms of social norms and expected behavior than might be the case in the East, where there is such a long tradition of philanthropy" (Lewin 2001).

The normative approach is complemented by the work of Havens and Schervish in developing a social psychological model of charitable giving based on the concept of identification and formulated from intensive interviews with

130 millionaires:

> Identification theory suggests that it is self-identification with others and with the needs of others (rather than *selflessness*) that motivates transfers to individuals and to philanthropic organizations and that leads givers to desire satisfaction from fulfilling those needs (2001:1).

Such identification with others may likely be fostered through a socialization process based on participation in a particular community and organization. As Schervish and Havens noted:

> for the population as a whole, participation, especially participation that already embodies a commitment to philanthropy as to a philanthropic organization, is directly related to giving behavior. Within community of participation, religious commitment and participation in religious organizations have a strong influence on general giving behavior (1997:255).

They continue: *"To understand giving behavior in the total population, it turns out one should focus on understanding the community of participation with special emphasis on the role of religious participation* (italics ours)" (1997:256). This observation is very consistent with the thrust of the present research.

Schervish and Havens concluded with the following observations, which support the research assumptions of this study:

> The basis for higher measured giving and volunteering may have less to do with generosity than with the density and mix of the network of formal and informal association within one's local community and the breadth of one's associations beyond the local level. This associational network reflects both the *willingness* of people to get involved as well as the *obligations* of involvement connected to certain types of engagements. Therefore, higher or lower levels of *measured* giving of time and money do not necessarily reflect differences in individual generosity. To understand these differences, we must look at the communal analog of what William Julius Wilson and others refer to as resources of social capital available to particular groups. When it comes to measured philanthropy, it is a matter not just of moral capital in the form of generosity. It is perhaps more a matter of *associational capital* in the form of social networks of invitation and obligation (1997:257).

Summary

Charity and philanthropy are conceptualized as part of the literature on gift exchange in society. Such gifts have reached extraordinarily high levels in recent years: $260 billion in 2005, representing 2.1 percent of GDP, with three-quarters of that sum coming from individuals. The largest beneficiaries of those charitable gifts were religious congregations and denominations, which received $93 billion or 36 percent of total contributions. That religion should receive the largest share of such contributions is not surprising since charity is a central tenet in the major religious traditions.

Substantial research in the behavioral sciences suggests that individuals may donate charity as a function of their consumer spending behavior (the economic explanation), or situational constraints (the psychological approach) or self-interest (the sociological and anthropological perspectives). Nevertheless, we suggest another possibility, a social psychological conceptualization: Individuals give charity when they participate in a culture and network of social relations that stress mutual interdependence and responsibility, especially when that culture has socialized them to identify with it.

Thus, relying on a social psychological perspective, the primary objective of this book is to understand and explain the motivations of individuals to make charitable gifts. To achieve this goal, a variety of data and methods will be employed as described in the next chapter, which draw on the perspectives of donors and non-donors as well as observations of directors of fundraising.

Notes:

1. For another international comparison, see Everatt, Habib, Maharaj, and Nyar (2005) on giving in South Africa, based on a quantitative survey.

2. See Hrung (2004) for differences between religious and non-religious giving.

3. These data are updated annually by the Giving USA Foundation, which may be contacted on-line at givingusa.org. As we went to press, media accounts indicated that total charitable donations in 2007 totaled $306.69 billion, which represented a 1 percent increase (adjusted for inflation) over the $294.91 billion contributed in 2006 (Strom 2008).

4. Leonhardt (2008) presents a popular examination of current economic explanations for why people give.

Chapter Two

Is Charity Caring Compassion or Social Justice?
The Case of the Jewish Community

> I read the mail last week, oh boy. On Wednesday came my fourth request from a dreaded disease foundation, this one accompanied by a handsome stack of return-address stickers. Next to it was the fifth letter from a local prison reform group asking for just a little bit more help, plus a fourteenth reminder from public television that my membership was running out. . . . Also stuffed in was my favorite of the week, a fourth request from some fellows in Western Massachusetts who are cornering the market on Yiddish books and want my support. *Oy vay!* (Press 1995:56).

Undoubtedly, many of us receive a multitude of requests. The aforementioned author claimed that he had received over one thousand solicitations in the calendar year, but how one responds to these requests may depend on how we conceive of charitable giving.

Caritas or *Tzedakah*? Caring Compassion or Social Justice

Fundamental to the initiatives in regard to philanthropy emanating from recent presidential administrations is the embedded Christian virtue of charity as formulated in the New Testament: "Though I speak with the tongues of men and of angels, and have not charity, I am become as sounding brass or a tinkling cymbal. . . . And now abideth faith, hope and charity, these three; but the greatest of these is charity" (1 Corinthians 13:1). Herein charity means *caritas*, love or caring compassion for another human being. In this sense, to offer charity is a religious virtue but not a legal obligation.

In contrast in Judaism, giving charity is a *mitzvah*, not a good deed as it is popularly translated, but a positive commandment or legal obligation to give to the poor. The cultural context is contained in the Hebrew word for charity, *tzedakah*,[1] which literally means justice or righteousness, and is similar to the cognate Arabic concept of *sadakah*. Thus, a gift of charity is transformed into a

19

"principle of justice" (Silber 2000:117). The distinction between charity and justice is referred to by Schoenfeld and Mestrovic (1989) in discussing *The Division of Labor in Society* by one of the European founders of sociology, Emile Durkheim (1933/1893). They noted that for Durkheim, the son of a rabbi, this distinction parallels the transformation from charity as the basis of morality in mechanical solidarity in small-scale societies to justice as the basis of morality in organic solidarity in large-scale societies (Schoenfeld and Mestrovic 1989:115). It may be that by combining the prevalent notion of caring compassion (as within a congregation in particular) with the principle of social justice (as within the community at large), American culture and society can more effectively address the underlying concerns which philanthropy seeks to ameliorate.

In rabbinic times in ancient Israel about two millennia ago, the system of charity was well-established and, after the Roman exile in the first century, continued to grow through the medieval period under the aegis of traditional Judaism. (See Lowenberg 1992, Neusner 1982, and Tamari 1987 for discussions of charitable giving in the Bible and Talmud.) The medieval period for Jews in Europe did not conclude with the Renaissance, but endured until the end of the eighteenth century. Modernity for Jews was ushered in by the French Revolution, which precipitated the collapse of the walls of the ghetto in which Jews were confined in many European communities. Even though traditional Judaism declined in popularity and power, first in Western Europe and North America and later in Eastern Europe, *tzedakah* maintained its place in the emergent new and less traditional denominations of Reform, Conservative, and Reconstructionist Judaism. (See Lazerwitz, Winter, Dashefsky, and Tabory 1998 on denominationalism.)

This concept of tzedakah, also noted by Mauss (1954/1925), "strongly connotes notions of righteousness and justice. . . . This was understood to mean, above all, that [t]zedakah is not an occasional favor done to the poor, but something that rightfully belongs to them, to which they are entitled. Rather than being left to the initiative of individuals, charitable giving was made into a matter of collective responsibility. . . ." (Silber 2000:125–26).

The greatest medieval Jewish philosopher, Moses Maimonides, taught that charity might be conceived of as a ladder and further instructed that even the poor must give tzedakah as noted in his *Mishneh Torah, Laws of Tzedakah*, 7:5 (cited by Isaacs 2005:28). See Figure 2.1 for the "The Ladder of Charity," based on Salamon's *Rambam's Ladder* (2003). In addition, a "paramount concern in the Jewish tradition . . . is the importance of [t]zedakah given in the proper manner, in the sense of avoiding shaming or humiliating the recipient" (Silber 2000:127). *The special attention to and elaborate codification of dealing with*

Figure 2.1 The Ladder of Charity

Responsibility: At the top of the ladder is the gift of self-reliance. To hand someone a gift or a loan, or to enter into a partnership with him, or to find work for him, so that he will never have to beg again.

Anonymity: To give to someone you don't know, and to do so anonymously.

Corruption: To give to someone you know, but who doesn't know from whom he is receiving help.

Boundaries: To give to someone you don't know, but allow your name to be known.

Shame: To hand money to the poor before being asked, but risk making the recipient feel shame.

Solicitation: To hand money to the poor after being asked.

Proportion: To give less to the poor than is proper, but to do so cheerfully.

Reluctance: To give begrudgingly.

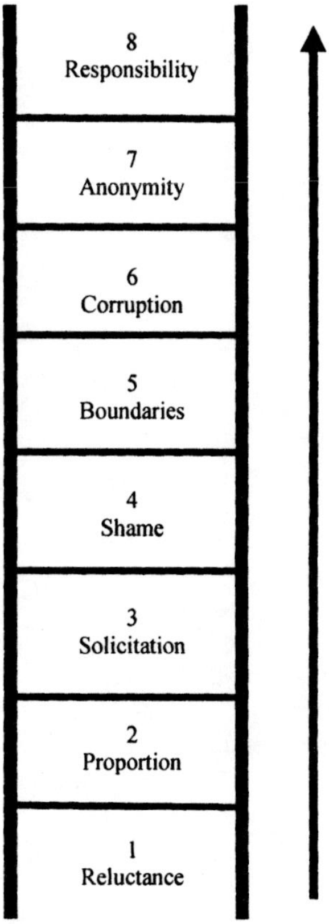

8 Responsibility
7 Anonymity
6 Corruption
5 Boundaries
4 Shame
3 Solicitation
2 Proportion
1 Reluctance

Note: Figure designed by Sam Richardson, based on Salamon (2003)

tzedakah in Jewish civilization has endured into the contemporary period although with some new twists. But does it work?

An examination of the Philanthropy 400 rankings in 2005, when the method was changed to provide data on all affiliated organizations, revealed that all 1,350 United Ways raised a combined total of $3.88 billion, followed by the Salvation Army at 1.55 billion, Food for Children at $888 million, American Cancer Society at $868 million, and AmeriCares at $801 million (www.philanthropy.com). The *Chronicle of Philanthropy* reported in regard to the United Jewish Communities the following:

> United Jewish Communities, an umbrella group for 155 Jewish federations, was the biggest of the entities that declined to submit consolidated information for all its local federations. If United Jewish Communities, No. 42 on the list, had provided complete data for all Jewish federations, it would have ranked second on the list, since it estimates that it raised $2 billion last year (Kerkman and Moore 2005).

In 1995, the total of all giving to United States Jewish philanthropies, including schools and synagogues, was estimated by Wertheimer (1997:40) at $4.2–4.4 billion dollars. No estimate was available for Jewish giving to non-Jewish charities, but in 2003 it was commonly observed that Jews gave more to non-Jewish charities than to Jewish ones. The proportion of Jews giving $100 or more to non-Jewish causes was 38 percent, to Jewish causes was 21 percent, and to the Jewish Federation campaign was only 10 percent (Cohen 2004:7). To illustrate further with dramatic examples, *Giving USA 2006* (AAFRC 2006:196) reported that among the four largest gifts in 2005 were $400,000,000 by the Hoffman, Rachofsky, and Rose families to the Dallas Museum of Art and $205,900,000 by George Soros to the Central European University. These donations derive from prominent and wealthy American Jews. By contrast, the first Jewish institution to appear on the list was the Jewish Communal Fund with a gift of $40,600,000 by Donald and Barbara Jonas (AAFRC 2006:197). Donations to non-Jewish causes like the art museum carry more prestige as they are recognized by the larger society. As Jews have become more assimilated and as anti-Semitism in the United States peaked during World War Two and has since generally declined, they have been more actively recruited by civic institutions, which formerly might have shunned them, and solicited for charitable gifts.

Thus, is Jewish charitable giving simply the result of a higher per capita income or are there normative patterns at work which encourage Jewish philanthropy even among more secularized Jews? This question begs for an examination of the Jewish case. Furthermore, Michael Steinhardt, a prominent philanthropist in the Jewish community, asserts that "the biggest gifts of 2002 ranged from $100 million to $375 million. Of the ten philanthropists, six were Jewish. Not a single one gave anything meaningful to a Jewish cause" (Steinhardt 2005:17).

Charitable Giving in the Jewish Community

Religion has set forth certain standards and expectations for its followers. To be sure, Judaism provides a wealth of information on the norms governing Jewish charitable behavior, or *tzedakah*, as found in the *Tanakh* or Hebrew bible, the fundamental basis of Jewish law. These norms are expanded and expounded upon in the *Talmud*, the second great literary work of Jewish civilization, which consists of sixty-three tractates of law and lore, spelling out the basis of ethical behavior. These works form the basis for Jewish religious law or the *halakhah* (literally the way or walk, i.e., the proper way to walk through life), which defines and integrates ritual and ethical behavior, including charity. In years past, *tzedakah* was well-integrated into the communal life of the Jews. In fact, both Jewish religious law and custom dictated traditions as to when and where there was a time to give. Thus while Jewish religious values mandated charitable behavior, communal institutions were developed to provide for the social and welfare needs of the people. *Tzedakah* was expected from all Jews so that, as Maimonides noted, even the poor are obligated to give charity; but the highest level of giving was to create conditions such that the poor would not need charity (see Figure 2.1).

Milton Goldin in his book, *Why They Give* (1976), documented the rich and sometimes colorful segment in American Jewish history of Jewish philanthropy, which arose to cope with the immigrant experience, dealing with a myriad of social, educational and health problems associated with an uprooted generation. What emerged were Jewish hospitals, old-age homes, loan societies and dozens of other agencies all needing financial support. The "Yahudim" (German Jews) had their "shtadlanim" (representatives with substance or "court" Jews) with their ability to raise large sums of money among themselves, while the "Yidn" (East European Jews) paid their dues, bought tickets to a variety of fundraisers, dinners, or theater benefits, and dropped their spare coins in "pushkas" (coinboxes). By 1915, "New York's *Jewish Communal Register* listed 3,637 institutions and agencies serving 1.5 million Jews" (Goldin 1976:64). To function efficiently and effectively, means had to be developed to coordinate fundraising. Indeed, in the early part of the twentieth century, a coalition of New York Jews sought to recapture the tradition of East European Jewry by creating a formal *kehillah* (or community) as described by Goren (1970). Another example of the transference of European traditions to the American Jewish experience is the study by Tenenbaum of Jewish loan societies in the United States, which reflected an "interaction of culture—the values and traditions that East European Jews brought with them—with contextual factors (e.g., economic opportunities) . . ." (1993:25). These works illustrate the extent to which tzedakah became communally based.

In addition to local needs, Jews felt a responsibility to co-religionists in other lands. News of pogroms in the Russian Pale, the dislocation in the aftermath of World War One, the unprecedented Holocaust, and the birth of the State of Israel have moved Jews to contribute their time, energy, and dollars in the name of *tzedakah*. These efforts in American society have led to the emergence of the local federation as the major instrument of Jewish philanthropy. For an excellent detailed examination of the scope of the American Jewish philanthropic structure, methods of fundraising, tax incentives for giving, amounts of Federation giving, as well as contributions to religious causes and other domestic and international charities, see Wertheimer (1997). The first local federation of Jewish charities emerged in Boston in 1895. Today there are 155 such Jewish federations in the United States and a network of 400 independent Jewish communities. The umbrella organization for all of them is the United Jewish Communities, created in 1999, as a merger of the United Jewish Appeal (founded in 1939 in the wake of Nazi attacks on Jews to help vulnerable coreligionists around the world) and the Council of Jewish Federations (founded in 1932 to provide services to the local Jewish Federations of North America) along with the United Israel Appeal (founded in 1925 to distribute funds raised by local UJA/Federation campaigns to support causes in Israel and the pre-state Yishuv or Jewish community in Palestine through the Jewish Agency for Israel). Elazar has noted:

> The Federation idea itself is a product of American Progressivism. The Federations were born during the height of the Progressive era [the first decades of the twentieth century until World War One]. They embodied the same understanding of efficiency and economy, philanthropic probity, community building, and civic involvement that characterized American progressives in all fields. Indeed, the Jewish community may have been the most successful of all American groups in its adoption and assimilation of Progressive ideas into its institutions and institutional culture. . . . This provided an excellent form for American Jews to adopt. The traditional *kehillah*, whose origins were in Babylonia in the sixth century BCE after the destruction of the First Temple, and which reached its apogee between the eleventh and fourteenth centuries, was autonomous and compulsory for all Jews. That is to say, Jews were recognized by their host nations as a nation in exile, subject to local rules, on one hand, but with substantial rights of self-government, on the other. . . .
>
> The *kehillah* system began to break down in the seventeenth and eighteenth centuries at the opening of the modern epoch as nation-states emerged and eliminated the idea of different laws for different groups in their boundaries in favor of the principle of one national law for all. Still, in Europe most Jews continued to be required to belong to their *kehillah* just as Christians were subject to the discipline of their churches. Only in the English-speaking world was this never the case because the Jewish communities in that world were entirely modern. Indeed, the most extreme example of this "free market" of identification was the United States. . . .
>
> The Federations were born as the Jews had relocated themselves in space from Europe to North America at a time when America was becoming a world power, and Progressivism was its dominant domestic ideal in a very different

cultural atmosphere than that which prevailed in America after World War One and that was again transformed in the 1960s. Consequently all of these locations have changed, even if our communities seem to be in the same general physical places that they were at the beginning of the twentieth century. For example, the space of "Chicago Jewry" is no longer simply in Jewish residential ghettos in Chicago, but is diffused throughout a metropolitan region only part of which is within the Jewish United Fund of Greater Chicago service area. . . .

After a century of looking toward government or public non-governmental activities for major initiatives, we have entered into an era of privatization. From federated giving, Federation's potential constituents have come to desire pinpointing their philanthropy and gain "hands-on" contact with the recipients of their contributions. Rather than seeking communal activities for their pleasure, they seek private ones, joining with the community only for certain kinds of "happenings" that appeal to them (2002:185).

Building on Elazar's work on the American Jewish polity, Woocher examines the civil religion of American Jews and states in his book, *Sacred Survival*:

The federations constitute . . . the "action arm" of the United Jewish Appeal, probably the single most widely visible and supported institution in American Jewish life. Thus, it is appropriate that this initial effort to define and to analyze the religion of the American Jewish polity takes the federation movement as its focus.

Sacred Survival traces the evolution of the guiding ideology of the movement from its origins as a value system emphasizing philanthropy and Jewish adjustment to American life to its current status as an encompassing set of beliefs which legitimate Jewish survival and activism in the modern world (1986:viii).

Tzedakah as the "Gift of Alms"

One very interesting study which documents the traditional practice of *tzedakah*, imported from Europe and applied to an American urban center, was carried out by Heilman (1975). The study is based on Heilman's participant observation in attending religious services at Kehillat Kodesh. He noted that, during the service, three types of mendicants would appear: the beggars, the "schnorrers," and the "meshulachim." Not all requests for money were met in the same manner. The beggar who had the lowest social acceptance did not stay for prayers, but rather provided the purpose for the daily charity box and allowed members to fulfill the commandment of giving. Yet the beggar did attest to the fact that this congregation was vital, as a beggar seldom chose to go to a "dying minyan" (or prayer quorum or group). Social bonding with beggars, however, was minimal.

The "schnorrers" were middle-class Jews who temporarily had come upon hard times. They appeared to take part in the service but in fact were "casing the joint." In this instance, the rabbi handled the transaction of money from donors to recipients. The "meshulachim" collected funds for others and tried to appear as guests, realizing that a strong sense of communal social bonding would yield more generous donations. They tried to involve the donors by assuring them that their contributions were important in that it was part of a larger goal (e.g., helping a school or Yeshiva).

While it may appear that gift-giving is spontaneous, voluntary, and done in a disinterested manner, Heilman observed that gifts were subject to rules of behavior. One gives not necessarily to the neediest (high dependency), but rather to those who have the most to give in return. If a beggar can in some way overcome his stigmatized appearance, then he will be more successful. Thus if the beggar can appear more as a stranger, he will be received in a better manner. Acceptance of the gift implied some expectation of repayment. Because the beggar was obviously unable to repay, he was heaped with degradation and jokes. If he appeared more fortunate, he symbolically would have affirmed the importance and wealth of the donor. The "schnorrer," however, was caught in the middle needing money, yet coming from a social position similar to the donor's. This left him open to feelings of shame and degradation. That is the reason why the rabbi acted as the go-between in transferring contributions.

The "meshulachim" presented themselves as having equal status with the donor, and they were sometimes rewarded with an invitation to participate in ceremonial rituals, an offer never extended to the beggars. Thus, the "meshulachim" sought social bonding in the hope of receiving larger gifts.

This study clearly documented that *tzedakah* is a ritualized behavior and part of the daily lives of the members of Kehillat Kodesh. Its roots were religious in origin, and it was evident that recipient and donor entered into a prescribed set of actions to fulfill the *mitzvah* (religious commandment) of *tzedakah*. Whether or not *tzedakah* takes on the same meaning outside of the Orthodox Jewish community is another question. But this question must be clearly addressed because education in traditional Jewish values seems a precipitant to elicit support for the numerous Jewish charitable institutions that have developed in the United States and abroad.

Changes in Jewish Giving Patterns

An early study found a demographic shift in giving, which foretold of changes that would become even more apparent in the recent past. Cohen (1979) relied on surveys gathered in 1965 and 1975 in the Jewish community of Boston. He found that there was a change in behavior and attitude toward early philanthropy from 1965 to 1975 in the Jewish community of Boston. Important to note was the difference in the age group of thirty to thirty-nine. In 1965, those making contributions rose sharply after the twenty to twenty-nine age group and the rate of giving also increased and remained high until age fifty. In contrast, ten years later, the giving rate for those entering the thirty to thirty-nine age group did not increase as dramatically as in 1965, with contributions gradually rising in each succeeding cohort, peaking in the age group of the fifties. "The more benign explanation suggests that, for some reason, by 1975 only middle-aged and elderly Jews regarded charitable giving as normative" (Cohen 1979:37). Another less benign reading may suggest that "the younger cohorts who began to mature between 1965 and 1975 were permanently less inclined to give than their predecessors. In other words, frequent giving is characteristic of only certain birth cohorts (according to these data, those born earlier than 1935)" (Cohen 1979:38). Another trend noted was that those who frequently gave were also more inclined to public and private Jewish behavior, such as synagogue attendance, lighting Sabbath candles, attending a Seder, and keeping a kosher home. In 1965, only 11 percent of those who gave most frequently were more likely to perform the above three rituals while in 1975 frequent donors were five times more apt to be performing these rituals. "It would appear that philanthropic activity has become increasingly confined to those Jews who regularly act out their Jewishness" (Cohen 1979:43).

A third change from 1965 to 1975 was found in patterns of employment. Self-employed professionals, a growing segment of the Jewish population, had begun to out-give the traditionally generous entrepreneurs. This was an important finding for two reasons. First, the rate of growth of professionals was not keeping up with the rate of decline in numbers of the entrepreneurs. Second, fundraisers reported that "super donors" were generally found among the affluent, self-employed business people and not among self-employed professionals. Central to this issue was the amount of disposability of income of self-employed and salaried professionals versus that of the entrepreneurs, the former being more limited than the latter. This early study foreshadowed trends that would only become more visible on a national level with the publication of the National Jewish Population Survey of 1990.

Indeed, some research does focus on variations across communities in the giving of charity. Tobin and Lipsman (1984), relying on data for eight metropolitan areas, found that the proportion claiming to contribute to Jewish causes ranged from a low of 63 percent in Miami to a high of 79 percent in Rochester. Sheskin examined data for thirty-nine communities and found that giving to Jewish charities ranged from a reported high of 95 percent in Boston in 1995 to 44 percent in Las Vegas also in 1995 (2001:191).

Identification or Affiliation?

We have seen that Jewish philanthropy is closely tied to the strength of Jewish identification and affiliation. But can a positive Jewish identity be maintained without formal membership? Can *tzedakah* exist without formal bonding? How one defines affiliation can be two-fold as Rabinowitz and Shapiro (1981) have pointed out in their study. There is the formal traditional method via the synagogue or communal organizations or the informal way via friendship relationships.

Two friendship networks of young Jews were explored to determine how the established Jewish communities could best involve these young people as the resources for the future. One friendship network evolved from a singles' group sponsored by the Jewish community. Therefore, their affiliation was already an established fact. The second group evolved on its own and consisted of young Jews who were non-joiners and individuals who found among themselves "mutual support, economic interdependence, social participation, social control and socialization" (Rabinowitz and Shapiro 1981:144). All of these needs traditionally may be met by a community.

While the second group of unaffiliated Jews may be viewed by the community at large as unconnected, their self-perception is one of affiliation and connection in an informal way with a group that has shared Jewish content and values. Another point worth considering is the method of outreach. *Fundraising is not the avenue of involvement and would be a waste of time and a turn-off for this group.* And yet, the Jewish community needs fresh ideas that can be gotten from such a group. Therefore, *the authors suggested that attempts must be made to attract these young people by offering them services that address their needs, such as marriage, parenting, or economic success.*

Conflict and Consensus in Allocation

These studies, especially Cohen's, emphasized the importance of positive Jewish identification with regard to Jewish philanthropy. In another early study of Jewish communities in San Francisco and San Diego, Weinberger (1972) added another dimension to the question of *tzedakah*. He was interested in determining whether leadership responsible for the allocation and distribution of charity dollars was in conflict or consensus with religious leaders and congregational presidents.

In each city, Jewish welfare leadership and religious leaders were asked to rank according to importance the various Jewish institutions. In San Francisco, religious leaders ranked the Jewish Education Bureau and the Jewish Day School one and two, with the Jewish Hospital and the Jewish Defense League seven and eight. Quite in contrast were the rankings of the leaders of the Jewish Welfare Fund in San Francisco, where decisions for allocating funds for all programs were made. They ranked the Jewish Hospital and the Jewish Community Center one and two in importance and gave a seven and eight for the Jewish Free Loan Society and the Jewish Day School respectively. From this finding, one is able to see that those community leaders who determined where charity dollars were being spent were widely divergent in their views from Jewish religious leaders. While this general finding about divergent perceptions may still be true, the Jewish Hospital and Day School may have been reversed in their rankings by most communal leaders in the contemporary period.

Central to the issue was the Jewish Hospital, which was not seen by religious leaders as enriching Jewish identity and, in fact, mainly served a non-Jewish population. In this community, it was the old established Jewish leaders of the Welfare Fund, making the largest contributions, who were making major allocation decisions; and they were not interested in looking for input from other segments of the population. Their choices reflected support for Jewish institutions which did not emphasize the particularistic but rather the universal contribution to the community like the hospital. It is interesting to note, however, that in 1971 a group of young concerned Jews staged a sit-in at the Federation office demanding an increase in allocations for Jewish education. This protest had positive results and increased dollars were spent on Jewish education.

In San Diego, a random survey which included a questionnaire and interview of twenty-four federation board members and twenty-nine modern Orthodox synagogue leaders showed more consensus about community priorities and funding allocations than in San Francisco. By comparison, the San Diego community was not raising as much money as in San Francisco; but the diversity in leadership was allowing for more consensus within the community. Programming was aimed at many different age-groups and leadership was very supportive of Jewish education. Newcomers were offered the opportunity to become involved in decision-making and contributions to Jewish philanthropy doubled between 1964 and 1967.

San Francisco represented the old established Jewish community with its Jewish Hospital being a major financial drain on resources. Its decision-makers were in conflict with those who saw Jewish survival primarily through Jewish education and institutions which emphasized the uniqueness of Judaism. San Diego represented the newer community that while not able to collect the amounts raised in richer areas, nevertheless showed awareness of the need to plan for the future by investing in institutions which fostered Jewish identity. This study highlights the transformation that the Jewish Federations underwent in the last third of the twentieth century, from an organization run by more secular Jews seeking more secure status in the general community to the present-day, emergent phenomenon of an organization administered by individuals with more religious motivations pursuing more particularistic objectives for the Jewish community.

Elite Jewish Philanthropy

By the 1990s, it was clear that in the preceding decades, an elite group of wealthy Jewish philanthropists had emerged. Odendahl (1990) studied 140 millionaires to better understand the social characteristics and personal attributes of the philanthropic elite. She also examined various groups of philanthropists including those with "old money" as well as self-made millionaires along with differences between men and women. In addition, she devoted a chapter in her book to "elite Jewish giving," where she highlighted generational differences by portraying three different givers: 1) a first-generation elderly Jewish man, 2) a second-generation middle-aged Jewish couple, and 3) a third-generation young Jewish woman. She summarized her observations as follows:

> Wealthy Jews of all generations in the United States have been faced with a dilemma. They have wanted to maintain their distinctive Jewish identity but at the same time to be accepted into the dominant, elite Protestant culture of philanthropy. This conundrum has affected Jews with old as well as new money. In spite of anti-Semitism, many Jewish people have become members and even leaders of the culture because of its constant need for money (Odendahl 1990:140).

She went on to summarize her observations about three generations of elite Jewish donors:

> There are generational differences among elite Jews. [The first generation] prefers to fund Jewish organizations. . . . The second generation . . . are large donors to the Jewish Federation, but they also give to virtually every cultural cause in New York. . . . The third generation . . . is not so sure what . . . Jewishness means. . . . [They] know that they are Jewish and rich but feel uncomfortable with both (Odendahl 1990:160).

These generational differences and tensions among the elite about their Jewish identity may very well be shared by the rank-and-file or the great majority of the Jewish community and they are emblematic of the assimilation of American Jews along with changes in Jewish identity and consequential patterns of Jewish charitable giving. Even though it is commonly assumed that 20 percent of donors give 80 percent of the dollars contributed to Jewish federations, these agencies recognize that they are not just raising money but building a community. Hence, understanding motivations for donations represent both a practical as well as theoretical concern.

Ostrower (1995) interviewed ninety-nine wealthy donors in metropolitan New York City to understand the sources of philanthropy and its role among community elites. Among those interviewed, eighty-eight were selected in a formal sampling procedure which resulted in 59 percent of the sample being Jewish, 26 percent Protestant, 10 percent Catholic and 4.5 percent with no religious affiliation. This disproportionate number of Jews in the sample was consistent with a study cited by Ostrower of 2,759 New Yorkers conducted by Sirota and Alper Associates. They found that for respondents with incomes of $100,000 or higher, 37 percent of Jews had contributed $5,000 or more in the preceding year while only 2 percent of Protestants and 11 percent of Catholics had done so. She also noted:

> The religiously affiliated pattern of giving among Jewish donors, however, diverged from the situation found elsewhere. . . . It involves huge sums of money contributed to a federated fund, although major elite philanthropy virtually never goes to umbrella organizations (1995:55).

Furthermore, she stated:

> Donors spoke of this gift as an obligation they felt they had as Jews. In doing so, their emphasis was on a sense of ethnic identity and membership in a particular community, rather than religiosity. . . . People spoke of giving to the Jewish affiliated fund as a "tax" that you simply pay as a member of the community (1995:56).

This notion of a communal "tax" seems to represent a cultural residue of the *kehillah* described earlier by Elazar (2002) above.

Finally, Ostrower observed:

> The issue of social pressure and fundraising in Jewish charities, however, is a complex one. In particular, while it might be tempting to conclude that Jewish philanthropy is the product of social pressure, such an explanation would be oversimplistic and indeed misleading. . . . It appears that those who participate to the extent of making their largest gifts to Jewish philanthropy generally view it as an obligation themselves, and thus do not feel they are responding to an externally imposed pressure even when they say they believe the pressure exists (1995:58).

Nevertheless, Ostrower noted that as more general cultural organizations and universities have courted Jewish contributors and invited them on their boards, this involvement appeared to lessen the level of donations to Jewish causes. Furthermore, these Jews who had entered New York's "social elite" revealed that class identity trumped religious and ethnic identity. All but one of these Jewish donors did not make their largest contribution to a Jewish affiliated organization. Still the Jews were different in political orientations. While four-fifths of the social elite were Republicans, a similar proportion among the Jews supported the Democrats.

Determinants of Giving and Identity

Thus far, our review of the literature has helped to situate Jewish charitable giving in its traditional European context (Heilman 1975), with the emergent demographic changes first noted by Cohen (1979), by noting the role of networks of relationships (Rabinowitz and Shapiro 1981), along with changes in attitudes and practices of Federation leaders (Weinberger 1972), and lastly in highlighting the emergence of Jewish philanthropy as part of the local community elite (Odendahl 1990 and Ostrower 1995). While several of these studies were qualitative in nature, more quantitatively based research was carried out by Ritterband, utilizing the 1981 Jewish Population Study of New York City. Ritterband (1991) addressed the issue of the determinants of giving and suggested "five issues of choice: identification with the recipient, moral commitment to give, identification with the community of givers, accessibility to the campaign, and dividing the pie" (1991:54). In examining the proportion of philanthropic dollars to Jewish causes, Ritterband noted:

> The most intriguing, surprising and disconcerting finding is the strong negative effect of household income. The higher the income, the lower the proportion given to Jewish causes. . . . The Jewish charities then, with their dependence upon big givers, face a twofold loss: 1) they participate in the general decline of giving characteristic of the American rich and 2) they lose a significant fraction of their gifts to non-Jewish campaigns (1991:69).

In another study (based on a community population survey (1986 MetroWest Federation of Morris and Essex Counties, New Jersey), Rimor and Tobin (1991) studied the relationship between Jewish identity and philanthropic behavior. They reported the following findings:

> Synagogue attendance and organizational membership associate directly with whether one contributes or not; synagogue and organizational membership and visiting Israel represent the sole predictors for the amount contributed. Religious practices, denominational affiliations, having Jewish friends, and years of Jewish

education, by contrast, are not associated directly with philanthropic behavior (1991:33).

Similarly, a British study reported a positive association between Jewish identity and charitable giving to Jewish causes:

- Non-givers comprised nearly one in four of the Secular and Just Jewish respondents . . . and this figure declined across the self-described religious outlook groups to only 3 percent of the Strictly Orthodox. . . .
- Fifty-two percent of the Secular favored only non-Jewish charities as compared with 7 percent of the Strictly Orthodox. . . .
- When asked to compare their top priority charitable category, 54 percent of the Secular group chose general British charities compared with 3 percent of the Strictly Orthodox. . . .
- [Only] 8 percent of the Secular Jews favored United Kingdom Jewish causes as compared with 80 percent of the Strictly Orthodox. . . .
- . . . The median donation for those who defined themselves as more British or as equally British and Jewish was £100; for those who felt more Jewish, it was £200 (Goldberg and Kosmin 1998:1).

Additional research on Jewish philanthropy emerged in the 1990s reflecting a greater involvement of women in fundraising. Gold (1997) conducted in-depth interviews with forty-seven individuals (including twenty women) from a wide variety of social backgrounds in both metropolitan Los Angeles and Detroit. One important finding that the study showed was that women differed from men in their approach to fundraising in the Federation world. Women were more interested in building relationships and men in seeking social status. This is a distinction observed by social psychologists even in games children play (Lever 1976). Girls tended to be more attuned to the socio-emotional side of social interaction in play whereas boys were more attuned to instrumental tasks in games. Nevertheless, the research reported that younger professional Jewish women found the Women's Division of the Jewish Federation less appealing than it was to more senior women even as the division was becoming more accepted in the Federation world. (For additional research on the issue of gender and giving, see Tress and Kosmin 1991, Goldstein 1991, and Monson 1991.)

While there was a growing body of research on Jewish philanthropy emerging in the last quarter of the twentieth century, very little relied on large nationwide probability samples. In Chapter Three, we will attempt to offset this limitation by examining data from the National Jewish Population Surveys.

An Overview of Data Sources

The aim of this study is to account for the charitable behavior of individuals by examining in particular the incentives and barriers to such giving. In this chapter, it is suggested that it would be useful to focus on the case of the Jews for several reasons.

First, the minority cultural matrix out of which giving stems reflects a communal concern with social justice, which is somewhat different from and perhaps complementary to the dominant cultural theme of caring compassion. Second, Jews are relatively well off economically so that a range of donations may be reflected in the community from very large "super-donors" to "non-givers," allowing for an examination of motivations for giving. Third, and most practical, there is, relatively speaking, an abundance of data available from national and local community studies, relying on both quantitative and qualitative methods, focusing on giving to the central Jewish fundraising agency, the Jewish Federation, which has emerged as an important communal institution derived from the established religious value of tzedakah.

Data for the current study were based on several sources:

1. The National Jewish Population Survey (NJPS) of 1970–71 (n=5,790, United Jewish Communities 1971) and NJPS 1990 (n=2,441, United Jewish Communities 1990) permit an analysis of the possible determinants of Jewish charitable giving. Some cursory references to NJPS 2000–01 (n=4,523, United Jewish Communities 2003) will be made; but a full comparison is not possible, owing to differences in the methods of gathering the data and the responses obtained, including declines in response rates from 79 percent in 1971 to 50 percent in 1990 to 28 percent in 2000–01.

2. A non-probability, purposive sample (n=72) of individuals, gathered by the coauthors in 1981–82 and drawn from a variety of geographic backgrounds (Florida, New England, New York, and Texas), allows for a more in-depth examination of motivations for giving by donors not captured in the large sample surveys that typically do not have the time to ask these questions. The sample was divided into three categories:

   a) *Donors* were givers (generally $500 or more) to the United Jewish Appeal (or UJA, one of the predecessor organizations to the United Jewish Communities or UJC created only in 1999) or to the local Jewish federation and, in addition, also synagogue members and/or members of two or more Jewish organizations.

   b) *Affiliated* were nongivers to UJA who were synagogue members and/or members of two or more Jewish organizations.

   c) *Unaffiliated* were nongivers to UJA who were neither members of synagogues or two or more Jewish organizations.

While a large nationwide probability sample provides a broad picture about a cross-section of the population, it cannot probe in-depth the various motivations for behavior. This kind of information can be investigated by collecting data from a smaller sample. Such a sample, based on in-depth interviews with seventy-two individuals, permitted an enriched examination of socialization and interpersonal factors that shape charitable giving as described in their own words. While the individuals specially interviewed for this study were not statistically representative of the entire American Jewish community, they were illustrative of the major patterns of affiliation with the UJA or local Jewish federation and Jewish organizational life—or the lack of it.

3.   A sample of directors of fundraising, conducted specially for this study, comprised the third major source of data. Personal in-depth interviews were carried out with more than two dozen professionals (n=25) who served as executive directors of local Jewish federations affiliated with the newer United Jewish Communities (UJC) or held national positions in Jewish fundraising organizations during 2000–03. These professionals in the local federations served in communities comprising more than three-quarters of the entire American Jewish population.

All of these data were assembled to address the following research questions:

   1.   *What are the motivations for charitable giving?*

   2.   *What are the prior socialization and current behavioral and attitudinal differences which separate the donors from those who do not give?*

   3.   *What are the perceived incentives and barriers to giving?*

   4.   *What are the current perceptions—both optimistic and pessimistic—of the directors of fundraising with respect to giving?*

The succeeding chapters will seek to answer these questions first by examining results from national probability samples and subsequently presenting findings from in-depth interviews with donors, potential donors and directors of fund-

raising. Hopefully, the answers will shed light on the complex interrelationship between motivations for philanthropic or charitable giving and changes in religious and ethnic identity.

Summary

In Chapter One, multiple approaches to understanding philanthropy or charitable giving, which may be shaped by overarching secular as well as religious paradigms, were discussed. In Chapter Two, the different approaches to charity of Christianity, emphasizing caring compassion to help others, and Judaism, emphasizing obligatory demands to practice justice, were noted. Despite the prevalence of economic, psychological, sociological, and anthropological explanations for charitable giving, referred to in Chapter One, an examination of the Jewish case may lead to a deeper knowledge of a normative or social psychological model of philanthropic behavior. A review of more than three decades of this kind of research revealed some interesting patterns as well as changes characterizing Jewish giving, which will be explored empirically with the three types of data sets available, including:

1. NJPS data especially 1970–71 (n=5,790) and 1990 (n=2,441) and some references to 2000–01 (n=4,523);
2. non-probability sample (n=72) of three groups of individuals including *Donors*, *Affiliated*, and *Unaffiliated* with respect to the Jewish community;
3. non-probability sample of professional directors of fundraising (n=25), who represented communities comprising more than 75 percent of the entire American Jewish population.

The next chapter will examine what can be learned from the large nationwide data sources mentioned above, namely, the National Jewish Population Surveys.

Note:
1. There are a variety of ways of transliterating or transcribing the Hebrew (and Yiddish) word, which may include the following: *s'daqa, ts'dokeh, tsedakah, tsedaqah, tsedoke, tz'daka, tz'dakah, tzedaka, zedaka,* or *zedakah.* We use the spelling most commonly seen in English.

Chapter Three

Sources of Philanthropic Giving:
Evidence from the
National Jewish Population Surveys

A tourist to a foreign country entered the premier concert hall in the capital for a tour and inquired of the guide: "Is this hall named after the famous prize-winning author?" "No," replied the tour guide, "it is named after a local person." "So," inquired the tourist of the guide, "what great work did your local author write?" To which, the tour guide replied, "A check!" While gifts of charity are generally viewed as generous, selfless acts, Mauss (1954/1925) and other social scientists noted that there is a payoff of some sort to the giver, although it may be viewed by some as in this world (i.e., social recognition or psychic gratification) or by some as in the next world (i.e., eternal salvation or a heavenly abode).

The National Jewish Population Survey (NJPS) permits an examination of the factors which shape the philanthropic giving of gifts. NJPS is a large, representative nationwide sample providing data on American Jewish contributions to the UJA/UJC (or local Jewish Federation) and other charities. In the current analysis (utilizing the 1990 survey as the benchmark), there were 1,905 respondents who represented a probability sample of American Jews. (Reference to the first NJPS of 1971 will be made subsequently as well as to the most recent or third NJPS of 2000–01, although a full comparison to the latter is not possible owing to a lack of comparability.)

While more than a decade and a half have passed since the release of NJPS 1990, it is most likely that the characteristics of its sub-groups and individuals have remained stable. Since the major trends in American Jewish life are the result of social processes that have been slowly working over decades, the characteristics of those who contribute or fail to contribute to the then UJA or local Jewish federation have most likely remained fairly similar in the past decade, an assumption largely substantiated in Chapter Seven. Hence, there is much to gain from a careful examination of the relationships among a variety of demographic, socioeconomic, and Jewish identification factors, including UJA involvement. (While the term UJA is used, it encompasses giving to the local Jewish federation, which represents the local affiliate of the relatively newly constituted entity, now called UJC, United Jewish Communities.) As noted in the previous chapter, the mid-range response rate of the 1990 NJPS makes it an especially valuable benchmark in moving both backward and forward in assessing trends in Jewish charitable giving.

Giving and Campaign Involvement

Table 3.1 gives the results of asking about respondent families' giving to their last local Federation/UJA drive. Overall, 45 percent claimed to have given. This is a high percentage of American Jewish adults and compares favorably with the

Table 3.1 Philanthropy of American Jews to Various Causes (NJPS 1990: "In 1989 did you and/or other members of your household together contribute, or give gifts?")

A. To the Jewish Federation or UJA?

Yes	No	Don't Know/Refused
45%	52%	3%

B. To Jewish philanthropies, charities, causes or other organizations?

Yes	No	Don't Know/Refused
63%	35%	2%

C. To philanthropies, charities, organizations or causes that are not specifically Jewish?

Yes	No	Don't Know/Refused
72%	26%	2%

47 percent of Jewish adults who claimed a synagogue membership in NJPS 1990. As reported in Chapter One by AAFRC (2002), 58 percent of all Americans belonged to a specific house of worship.

An even greater percentage of respondent families (63 percent) also claimed to have given to other local Jewish community fund drives. Finally, 72 percent of these families claimed to have given to non-Jewish charity drives, a figure not very different from the 70 percent of all Americans who contributed to religious causes, as reported in Chapter One by AAFRC (2002). A greater portion of American Jews gave to non-Jewish charity drives than to general Jewish causes or the UJA specifically, dispelling the notion that Jewish giving is only parochial. *Nevertheless, Jews did not appear to give in greater proportions than other Americans; but they did appear to give in greater amounts as noted in Chapter Two. Why this is so is an interesting question that few studies seem to address empirically. The assumption herein is that a normative cultural obligation of tzedakah, coupled with a network of community ties, supported by above average income, and a possible sense of greater political and social insecurity occasioned by the anti-Semitism of the past (e.g., the Holocaust) or the present circumstances of Jewry in Europe and the Middle East, supports Jewish philanthropic generosity.*

Fewer Jewish adults (24 percent) claimed to have done volunteer work in their local Jewish fund drives, as seen in Table 3.2. Furthermore, a still larger percentage of Jewish adults (41 percent) claimed to have worked for their local,

Table 3.2 Volunteering of American Jews to Jewish and Non-Jewish Organizations (NJPS 1990: "During the past 12 months have you done volunteer work yourself or as part of a group?")

A. For a Jewish Organization?

Yes	No	Don't Know/Refused
24%	76%	0%

B. For a Not Specifically Jewish Organization?

Yes	No	Don't Know/Refused
41%	59%	0%

Table 3.3 Gave to UJA by Giving to General Charities

Giving to
General Charities

Gave to UJA	Yes	No	Total
Yes	38%	7%	45%
No	34%	21%	55%
			100%

general (not Jewish) charity fund drives. In Table 3.3, one sees that 38 percent have given to both Jewish and non-Jewish fund drives. Seven percent gave to the Jewish but not to the general fund drive; 34 percent gave to the general, but not Jewish fund drives; and 21 percent gave to neither.

A Model of Jewish Giving

One of the objectives of this book is to better understand the factors that encourage as well as impede charitable giving by focusing on one group, American Jews, and the way they practice philanthropy. Obviously, they can give their financial resources to a wide variety of institutions. Within the Jewish community, the central fundraising and dispensing organization has been the local Jewish federation. Hence, the first question of interest is giving to the local Jewish federation. This question obviously must be followed by one that asks about financial giving to other Jewish philanthropies, charities, causes, or other organizations. These two questions exhaust giving within the Jewish community. Naturally, these questions lead to one about giving to non-Jewish philanthropies, charities, organizations, or causes. But it is possible to give of one's time in place of money. This requires questions that ask about volunteer work for Jewish organizations and about volunteer work for non-Jewish organizations. These combinations of financial giving or giving of oneself cover all aspects of the ways of giving to one's community.[1] Therefore, these questions form the dependent variables to be examined in the Jewish community: 1) gave to UJA, 2) gave to other Jewish charities, and 3) volunteer work in Jewish voluntary associations; and in the larger non-Jewish community: 4) gave to non-Jewish charities, and 5) volunteer work in general associations. A host of independent variables are examined to develop explanations for the variations in these dimensions of charitable giving.

Wertheimer (1997), in his excellent review of trends in American Jewish philanthropy and following up on Cohen's earlier review (1979), identified a number of key variables that affect giving, including demographic factors, socioeconomic status, and Jewish identification. This section assesses the impact of a variety of such independent variables on giving to UJA, other Jewish charities, and volunteering for Jewish causes as well as giving to non-Jewish charities and volunteering for general causes. The statistical technique used in this section is multiple regression analysis. This technique enables a determination of the influence of one variable on another while holding statistically constant the influence of other variables. The first step in such an analysis is to specify the order in which the variables are to be entered into the statistical equations. Those that appear early in the equation serve as controls. That is, their influence is held constant statistically when looking at the influence of the variable of central concern.

The resulting analyses provide two statistics of interest: the standardized coefficient of regression value (beta), and the squared multiple correlation coefficient (R^2). Beta, the standardized coefficient of regression, indicates how much a dependent variable changes for each unit of change in one of its independent variables above and beyond the impact, or influence, of any other independent variable. The squared multiple correlation coefficient, or R^2, indicates how much of the variation of a dependent variable is explained by the combined impact of all the independent variables of a regression equation. For an elaboration of this statistical technique, refer to Sonquist, Baker, and Morgan (1971), Andrews and Messenger (1986, 1973), Andrews, Morgan, and Sonquist (1969) and Blalock (1969 and 1979).

The independent variables that were used, in order of their appearance in the relevant equations, are:

1. *Demographic,* namely: gender, age, marital status together with the number of minor children in the household (called life cycle), and the number of generations which one's family has been in the United States;
2. *Socioeconomic,* such as the level of secular education, the occupation of the family head, and family income;
3. *Religious,* for example, the years of Jewish education in one's youth, current denominational preference, and synagogue membership.

These variables were selected due to the hypothesized influence they may have on charitable giving. For example, the demographic variables chart differences in generation or age that may influence charitable giving, with younger people and more assimilated generations giving less. Likewise, socioeconomic status, particularly income, may be associated with higher levels of giving. Finally, religious variables may show that the more traditional and pious individuals are, the more likely they are to make charitable contributions. By placing these three sets of variables first in the equation, the influence of demographic and socioeconomic factors as well as of Jewish education, denomination, and synagogue membership are statistically controlled. This statistical technique enables one to determine which variables relate to aspects of the respondents' Jewish and non-Jewish involvements above and beyond the influence of demographic characteristics, socioeconomic status, and these initial Jewish background factors. The particular aspects of the respondents' Jewish involvement that are of interest follow: attendance at religious services, religious practices at home, involvement with Jewish primary groups, activity in Jewish voluntary associations, and orientation toward Israel.

What do the components of the model tell us? First, in examining the demographic variables of gender, age, generations in the United States, and life cycle, Table 3.4 shows that for giving to the UJA or other Jewish charities, or activity in voluntary Jewish associations, women were slightly more involved than men. However, only for voluntary association activity did gender reach a moderate level of impact, with women being significantly more active than men. In regard to age and giving to the UJA or other Jewish charities, the older the respondent, the more the giving. The impact on the UJA was strong, while for other Jewish charities, the impact was a bit lower. Age, however, had no effective impact on activity in Jewish voluntary associations. The other two demographic variables, generations in the United States and life cycle, had only weak impacts on giving and activity.

For the package of socioeconomic variables, education, occupation of family head, and family income provided an interesting picture. Neither education nor occupation had any meaningful impacts. It was income that had moderate impacts on the two giving variables to no one's surprise. But income did not affect volunteer activity in Jewish associations.

In regard to the "Jewish variables," Jewish education had only a weak impact on giving to the UJA, but moderate impacts on giving to other Jewish charities and voluntary association activity. Denomination had a moderate impact on giving to the UJA with adherents of the Conservative and Reform denominations most likely to give. Based on evidence from Lazerwitz, et al. (1998), members of these denominations had higher incomes than the Orthodox and non-members.

Synagogue members were quite likely to give and to be active. Those who attended synagogue more frequently were more likely to give to various Jewish

Table 3.4 Betas and Squared Multiple Correlations of the Jewish Charity Contributions Model, NJPS 1990

	Demographic Variables					Socioeconomic Variables		
Dependent Variables	Gen- der	Age	U.S. Gener	Life Cycle		Educ	Head Occup	Family Income
a. Gave to UJA	-.05	.21	-.04	.04		.03	-.01	.11
b. Gave to other Jewish Charities	-.05	.18	.07	.02		.01	.03	.14
c. Volunteer Worker in Jew- ish Vol. Assoc.	-.10	.04	.06	.04		.01*	.04	.04

Jewish Variables

Dependent Variables	Jewish Education	Denom	Syn Memb	Syn Attend	Home Religious Practice	Jewish Primary Groups	Israel Orient	R^2
a. Gave to UJA	.08	.10	.16	.09	.06	.16	.14	.31
b. Gave to other Jewish Charities	.10	.07	.11	.12	.13	.12	.09	.33
c. Volun- teer Work- er in Jew- ish Vol. Assoc.	.12	.02	.15	.20	.03	.08	.08	.24

Notes: An asterisk means beta category values are not monotonic. A minus sign means (a) the smaller the independent values, the larger the dependent value; or, (b) for gender, men have smaller or less traditional values than women.

The values in this table may be interpreted as follows: Values less than .10 mean that the given independent variable has little or no influence on one of the (3) dependent variables. Values of .10-.19 have a moderate effect and values of .20 and larger have a strong impact.

charities and a lot more likely to have been active in Jewish voluntary associations. The performing of more home religious practices had a moderate impact only on giving to other Jewish charities. Those more involved in Jewish primary groups were more likely to give to the UJA and other Jewish charities. Finally, being Israel-oriented was associated with a moderate impact on giving to the UJA. There was a solid amount of overall variance explained for the two giving variables and somewhat less for volunteer work in Jewish associations.

Summarizing these findings of Table 3.4 shows that giving to the UJA or other Jewish charities was associated with age, income, Jewish education, denomination, synagogue membership, synagogue attendance, involvement with Jewish primary groups, home religious practice, and being oriented toward Israel. Being active in Jewish voluntary associations was associated with being a woman, more Jewish education, synagogue membership, and more frequent synagogue attendance.

Table 3.5 focuses on giving to non-Jewish charities and doing volunteer work for general (not Jewish) community voluntary associations. Generation in United States was the only demographic variable to have even a moderate impact. The more generations in the United States, the more likely to give to charities that were not Jewish, indicating a degree of greater assimilation. In addition, education had a moderate impact on giving and general volunteer work. Family income, as would be expected, had a moderate impact on giving to non-Jewish charities.

Denomination had a moderate impact on volunteer activity in general associations. Those without a denominational preference were the most likely to be active followed by those who preferred the Conservative and Reform denominations. The Orthodox were the least likely to volunteer their efforts for general community voluntary associations.

Synagogue membership, synagogue attendance, or home religious practices all had weak impacts on both dependent variables. Jewish primary group involvement had a moderate impact on volunteer work in general community associations. However, the impact was a negative one: the less involvement in Jewish primary groups, the more volunteer work for general community associations. Being active in Jewish organizations and giving to Jewish charities had moderate impacts on giving to non-Jewish charities, while actually doing volunteer work for Jewish organizations had a moderate impact on volunteer work in general community associations. Also, these regression equations accounted for the least variance of the full set of five regressions presented in Tables 3.4 and 3.5.

The regression equation for giving to non-Jewish charities shows that activity in Jewish community associations and giving to Jewish charities both had moderate impacts upon giving to non-Jewish charities. For this regression equation, the variance explained increases to .18 from the .13 of the other regression equation, which accounts for volunteer work as an area of philanthropic activity.

Table 3.5 Betas and Squared Multiple Correlations of the Non-Jewish Charity Contributions Model, NJPS 1990

	Demographic Variables					Socioeonomic Variables		
Dependent Variables	Gender	Age	U.S. Gen	Life Cycle		Educ	Head Occup	Family Income
a. Gave to Non-Jewish Charities	-.05	.08	-.10	.06		.16	.06	.12
b. Volunteer Work in General Assoc.	0	.05*	-.08	.02	.	.15	.03*	.01

Jewish Variables

Dependent Variables	Jewish Educ	Denom	Syn Memb	Syn Attend	Home Religious Practice	Jewish Primary Groups	Israel Orient	Jewish Org Activity	Jewish Vol Work	Give Jewish Charity	R^2
a. Gave to Non-Jewish Charities	.03	-.07	-.02	.06*	-.07	-.03	.03*	.17	–	.14	.18
b. Volunteer Work in General Assoc.	.02	-.12	.02	.06*	-.02	-.17	.04*	.02	.16	–	.13

Notes: An asterisk means beta category values are not monotonic. A minus sign means (a) the smaller the independent values, the larger the dependent value; or, (b) for gender, men have smaller or less traditional values than women.

The value in this table may be interpreted as follows: Values less than .10 mean that the given independent variable has little or no influence on one of the two dependent variables. Values of .10-.19 have a moderate effect and values of .20 and larger have a strong impact.

Just how good are the predictors obtained by these regression equations? The regression equation calculations also give tables showing how well they predict those who actually did contribute or did volunteer work and those who did not. For Tables 3.6A and 3.6B, the predictions correspond quite well to reality. For giving to the UJA, Table 3.6A correctly predicted actual giving 73 percent and not giving 75 percent of the time. For giving to other Jewish charities, Table 3.6B predicted actual giving 87 percent of the time and this proportion drops down to 62 percent for those who did not give. However, for Table 3.6C, the ability to predict volunteering to work in Jewish organizations falls apart. It certainly did very well on predicting the failure to volunteer, but only 36 percent of those who did volunteer were predicted to have done this.

Tables 3.6D and 3.6E show predicted giving to non-Jewish charities or volunteering to work for non-Jewish associations. In Table 3.6D, actual giving is predicted exceedingly well with 94 percent who actually gave; but not giving is correctly predicted in just 29 percent of the cases. Table 3.6E shows the prediction of volunteering to work. The regression equation fails to predict actual volunteering half of the time; however, it does predict not volunteering in 78 percent of the cases.

Overall then, prediction is good for giving to the UJA and other Jewish charities. It is excellent for giving to non-Jewish charities, but fails to do a good job of predicting not giving for this variable. However, the "volunteering to work" equations do not work well. Only *not* volunteering for the non-Jewish associations is done with a high degree of accuracy.

With all these efforts concluded, it can be stated that the statistical patterns show that giving to Jewish causes was associated with aging and family income. Then, involvement in the life of the organized Jewish community entered in with synagogue membership, synagogue attendance, home religious practices, involvement in Jewish primary groups, and an orientation toward Israel—all combining to reinforce giving to Jewish charities (including the UJA).

More than assimilation being a significant factor (as measured by United States generation, i.e., the more generations in the United States the less giving), variables like aging and family income, along with Jewish communal involvement through formal and informal networks sustained giving to the UJA and other Jewish charities. Nevertheless, as the prediction tables showed, fewer factors predicted volunteer activity in Jewish associations. Women, more Jewish education, and the role of the synagogue (in terms of denominational preference and membership) were the dominating factors. Note that again synagogue membership and attendance counted. For giving to non-Jewish charities, activity in Jewish organizations and giving to Jewish charities were both associated with giving to non-Jewish charities. Also, the factors of more generations in the United States, more education, and more family income played important roles.

Table 3.6A Predictability of Giving to UJA

	Predicted Giving	Predicted Not Giving
Actually Gave	73%	27%
Actually Did Not Give	25%	75%

Table 3.6B Predictability of Giving to Other Jewish Charities

	Predicted Giving	Predicted Not Giving
Actually Gave	87%	13%
Actually Did Not Give	38%	62%

Table 3.6C Predictability of Volunteering in Jewish Associations

	Predicted Volunteering	Predicted Not Volunteering
Actually Volunteered	36%	64%
Actually Did Not Volunteer	7%	93%

Table 3.6D Predictability of Giving to Non-Jewish Charities

	Predicted Giving	Predicted Not Giving
Actually Gave	94%	6%
Actually Did Not Give	71%	29%

Table 3.6E Predictability of Volunteering in Non-Jewish Associations

	Predicted Volunteering	Predicted Not Volunteering
Actually Volunteered	51%	49%
Actually Did Not Volunteer	22%	78%

Volunteering for work in non-Jewish voluntary associations was associated with more education. It was also associated with volunteering for work in Jewish associations as well as being marginal to the organized Jewish community. For example, those who had no denominational preference nor synagogue membership were the most likely to volunteer for non-Jewish organizations with those who considered themselves Orthodox the least likely to do this particular kind of volunteering. Finally, those who were least involved with Jewish primary groups were more inclined to do such volunteering. *In short, activity in the Jewish sector is also associated with activity in the non-Jewish sector. However, those who were weak in their involvement with the organized Jewish community were more likely to be involved with the non-Jewish sector.*

Jewish Charitable Giving in Retrospect

What additional insights as to the relationship between religio-ethnic involvement and charitable contributions can be gained by going back in time to the National Jewish Population Survey of 1971? In trying to answer this question, this earlier survey will be analyzed and then compared to the 1990 survey in order to understand better the direction of change across time.

The frequent problem in dealing with two or more surveys is the difference in the wording of the survey questions. This problem emerges as the wording about who gave a contribution is different. For example, the question wording in the 1990 survey was: "In 1989 did you and/or other members of your household together contribute or give gifts to. . . ." The question wording in the 1971 survey was: 1) "In 1969 did (Head) contribute to the Jewish. . . ." 2) "In 1969, I contributed to the Jewish. . . ." In other words in the 1990 survey, the "giving questions" pertained to the entire household, be it the head or the randomly selected Jewish respondent, or anyone else living there. In the 1971 survey, the "giving questions" pertained to the head of the family or the randomly selected

Jewish respondent, not the entire household. (In the 2000–01 NJPS, the data applied to the households.)

In the analysis of the data from the 1990 survey, the randomly selected adult respondents have their characteristics joined to household contributions. In the analysis of the data from the 1971 survey, the randomly selected adult respondents have their characteristics joined to their own contributions, together with a limited number of household questions, such as occupation of family head and total family income.

Tables 3.7 and 3.8 give the percentages of household heads and randomly selected respondents in 1969 who claimed to have given to the UJA, their local Jewish federations, or their local general community fund drives. Table 3.9 gives the percentage of respondents who claimed to have been active as volunteers in these fund drives.

Table 3.7 Philanthropy of American Jewish Family Heads to Various Causes (NJPS 1971: "In 1969 did family head contribute to . . . ?")

A. The United Jewish Appeal (UJA)

Yes	No	Don't Know/Refused
45%	37%	18%

B. Other Jewish Campaigns

Yes	No	Don't Know/Refused
57%	22%	21%

C. The General (not Jewish) Central Community Campaign

Yes	No	Don't Know/Refused
70%	12%	18%

Table 3.8 Philanthropy of American Jews to Various Causes (NJPS 1971: "In 1969, I contributed to. . . ?")

A. The United Jewish Appeal (UJA)

Yes	No	Don't Know/Refused
64%	38%	8%

B. Other Jewish Campaigns

Yes	No	Don't Know/Refused
48%	41%	11%

C. The General (not Jewish) Central Community Campaign

Yes	No	Don't Know/Refused
63%	29%	8%

Table 3.9 Volunteering of American Jews to Jewish and Non-Jewish Organizations (NJPS 1971: "In 1969, I was active as a volunteer in. . . ?")

A. A Jewish Fundraising Campaign

Yes	No	Don't Know/Refused
13%	82%	5%

B. A General (not Jewish) Fundraising Campaign

Yes	No	Don't Know/Refused
13%	81%	6%

In 1971, 45 percent of family heads and 64 percent of respondents claimed to have contributed to the UJA. Also, 57 percent of heads and 48 percent of respondents claimed to have contributed to their local Jewish charities apart from the UJA. Also in 1971, 70 percent of heads and 63 percent of respondents claimed to have contributed to their local general (not Jewish) charity fund drive. Finally, as seen in Table 3.9, just 13 percent of respondents claimed to have been volunteers in their Jewish or general fund campaigns.

Table 3.10 introduces the model for contributions to the UJA in the 1971 survey. For the most part, the beta values are weak. However, generation in the United States had a negative association with giving to the UJA. As the number of generations in the United States increased, the percentage giving decreased, especially after the first two generations in the United States. Life cycle had a strong association with giving to the UJA. The denomination variable had a moderate association with giving to the UJA, with a drop in percentage giving to it among those who preferred the Reform denomination or who had no denominational preferences. The more home religious practices or the more involvement in Jewish primary groups, the more individuals gave to the UJA. Finally, synagogue attendance displayed an inconsistent relationship to giving to UJA.

Table 3.11 presents the findings on the model of general (not Jewish) giving. Number of United States generations had barely a moderate impact on giving. The lowest contribution was for the first generation; then, contributions peaked in the second generation. After this, there was a small drop and a leveling off. Age and life cycle had considerable impacts. With age, there was a constant drop-off, with those in the oldest group claiming to be more likely to have given followed by the middle-age group. The young were the least likely to claim giving. As would be expected, the more income individuals had at their disposal, the more likely they were to give.

As to Jewish characteristics, both Jewish education and denominational preference had inconsistent connections with giving. Apart from Jewish organizational activity, the other Jewish factors had weak impacts with the World Jewry-Israel orientation variable, being both weak and inconsistent. Nevertheless, activity in Jewish organizations had a moderate, positive impact on giving to non-Jewish charities. The more such Jewish activity, the more likely respondents claimed to have given. This connection of prior activity in Jewish philanthropy and subsequent contributions to non-Jewish charities was clearly documented by York (1979).

How good is the predictability of these two models? This is examined in Tables 3.12A for giving to the UJA and 3.12B for giving to general charities. Clearly both tables are quite similar. Practically every respondent who in the 1971 model was predicted to have given actually gave to the UJA and general charities. However, it is much more difficult to handle those 1971 respondents who did not give. On both "giving" variables, there is about a fifty-fifty split on not giving.

Table 3.10 Betas and Squared Multiple Correlations of the Jewish Charity Contributions Model, NJPS 1971

	Demographic Variables					Socioeconomic Variables		
Dependent Variables	Gender	Age	U.S. Gen	Life Cycle		Educ	Head Occup	Family Income
a. Gave to UJA	0.3	.06	-.12	.20	.	.03	.06	.08

Jewish Variables

Dependent Variables	Jewish Education	De-nom	Syn Memb	Syn Attend	Home Religious Practice	Jewish Primary Groups	World Jewry & Israel	R^2
a. Gave to UJA	.04	.10	.02	.10	.14	.11	.04	.28

Table 3.11 Betas and Squared Multiple Correlations of the Non-Jewish Charity Contributions Model, NJPS 1971

	Demographic Variables					Socioeconomic Variables		
Dependent Variables	Gender	Age	U.S. Gen	Life Cycle		Educ	Head Occup	Family Income
a. Gave to Non-Jewish Charities	.04	.18	.10	.20	.	-.05	.06	.14

Jewish Variables

Dependent Variables	Jewish Education	De-nom	Syn Memb	Syn Attend	Home Religious Practice	Jewish Primary Groups	World Jewry & Israel	J. Org. Activ.	R^2
a. Gave to Non-Jewish Charities	.12*	.08*	-.02	.07	-.03	.01	.08*	.16	.18

Table 3.12A Predictability of Giving to UJA in 1969

	Predicted Giving	Predicted Not Giving
Actually Gave	93%	7%
Actually Did Not Give	50%	50%

Table 3.12B Predictability of Giving to General Charities in 1969

	Predicted Giving	Predicted Not Giving
Actually Gave	91%	9%
Actually Did Not Give	54%	46%

Contrasting Two NJPS Models

The period from 1971 to 1990 saw a considerable change in the characteristics of the American Jewish population. As reported by Lazerwitz, et al. (1998:72, Table 4-3), American Jewry underwent moderate increases in synagogue attendance and religious practices performed at home in those two decades. On the other hand, there was also a strong decrease in involvement in Jewish primary groups and moderate decreases in Jewish and general voluntary association activities.

The contrast of the two models for contributions to the UJA in each of the two survey years also showed a number of important changes. Between 1971 and 1990, both United States generations and family life cycle variables changed from influential variables to weak ones. Age, on the other hand, went from being a weak variable in 1971 to having a strong impact by 1990. The older respondents were more likely to have someone in their household who gave to the UJA. Also, the impact of family income showed some increase between the two surveys.

In addition, synagogue membership increased from weak to a moderate impact variable. Home religious practices went from a moderate impact variable to a weak one. Jewish primary group involvement strengthened its impact.

What about the models with regard to contributions to general charities? From 1971 to 1990, age dropped from being a moderate to a weak impact variable. Life cycle went from being a strong impact variable to a weak one. By 1990, education emerged as a moderate impact variable from having been a weak one in 1971.

For giving to general charities, by 1990 the dominant independent variables were related to socioeconomic status, education and family income, together with activity in Jewish voluntary associations. However for giving to the UJA, it was the Jewish communal involvement variables that dominated by 1990 as noted above. Tied in with this pattern was higher income that was also associated with being older.

NJPS 2000–01

In each of the previous two NJPS analyses, different strategies were followed in the design of the study, including relying on questions with slightly varied wording, as well as constructing sampling frames based on different strategies which produced response rates successively lower comparing 1971 to 1990 as cited in the previous chapter. For example, the response rate in 1971 was 79 percent and in 1990 it was 50 percent. The latter relied on telephone interviews based on Random Digit Dialing (RDD) and the former utilized face-to-face interviews in a "multistage, clustered, stratified sample design" (Lazerwitz et al. 1998:178).

The most recent NJPS of 2000–01 also relied on RDD, but for a variety of reasons produced a much lower response rate of 28 percent to the screening interviews with a 40 percent cooperation rate. The challenge of gathering data on a representative sample of American Jews is that they are a very small percentage of the American population, equaling approximately 1.8–2 percent in 2000 (see Sheskin and Dashefsky 2007). That is about half of the proportion they were in the 1930s. In sum, Jews are a "rare population," and gathering data on Jewish people poses great challenges of time and money.

As noted earlier, philanthropic giving among American Jews is relatively generous compared to other religious groups, but it is by no means uniform. Cohen (1979), as previously stated, found a demographic shift in Boston, which suggested the possibility that certain birth cohorts were less likely to contribute. Based on an analysis of NJPS 2000–01, Cohen (2004) examined the question of who gives and how much. He reported the following results:

- Jews living in the West are less likely to give to Federations than Jews residing in other regions of the country.
- The association between Jewish institutional affiliations and contributions is stronger for Federation giving than for giving to other Jewish and non-Jewish causes.
- People with higher household incomes give more of their charitable dollars to Federations than those with lower incomes.

- Those born after 1950, who are today middle-aged or younger, display
  a more significant drop-off in Federation giving than in contributions to
  other causes (2004:1).

The age gap in giving, particularly to Federations, may be the result of individuals being in different stages of the "life cycle" or the result of the year in
which they were born ("cohort effect") as Cohen noted: "Those born after 1950
did not change their giving patterns to resemble those born before 1950; this is
consistent with birth cohort rather than a life cycle explanation" (Cohen 2004:8).

In sum, NJPS 2000–01 found that the variables which had the most pronounced effect on greater Federation giving were *age* (born before 1950), *income, institutional affiliations,* and *region* (with Westerners less likely to give).
Despite the methodological variations among the three NJPS panels, the findings are rather similar. Nevertheless, the earlier two studies also found that home
religious practices, involvement in Jewish primary groups, and a positive orientation to Israel also increased Jewish charitable giving.

Regional differences were found in the earlier two NJPS studies. Lazerwitz
(1977) reported that in the 1971 survey, residents of Los Angeles and other larger Jewish communities, including Boston, ranked lower on Jewish identification
than the residents of other Jewish communities. Similarly, NJPS 1990 revealed
that the largest segment of secular Jews (with no religion) was in the West
(somewhat greater than in the Northeast and nearly twice as great as in the South
and nearly three times as in the Midwest).

In contrasting the three survey years with regard to giving to Federation (or
UJA), the latest NJPS found only 30 percent of households had contributed
(United Jewish Communities 2003:13), down from 45 percent in 1971 and 1990.
In addition, giving to other Jewish causes had decreased to about two-fifths of
the population (41 percent), down from about three-fifths in the earlier surveys
(1971=57 percent and 1990=63 percent). Finally, donating to a non-Jewish
cause was also down to 62 percent in 2000–01 compared to 70 percent in 1971
and 72 percent in 1990. While differences in question wording might account
for some variation, it seems as though the demographic and sociological changes
producing more assimilation among American Jews were lessening their pro-
pensity to contribute to both Jewish and general causes, a trend most noticeable
in the decade since 1990.

These patterns of the general decline in Jewish giving to Jewish causes is
most dramatically seen among high-end givers. Tobin summarizes the situation
as follows:

> At the highest end of giving, donations of $10 million or more, Jews are dis-
> proportionately represented, making 23 percent of all such gifts. Only 6 per-
> cent of Jewish mega-gifts go to Jewish institutions. The lion's share goes to

college and arts and culture. . . . Approximately $8-10 billion annually is directed into Jewish institutions including . . . synagogues (Tobin 2004:31).

See also Tobin, Solomon, and Karp (2003).

Summary

The two NJPS surveys of 1971 and 1990 provided comparable, quality data on the variables associated with giving to and activities in charitable funding. Overall, age, family income, Jewish education, denominational preference, synagogue membership and attendance, involvement in Jewish primary groups, home religious practices, and a positive orientation toward Israel formed the normative factors that increased both giving to and activity in Jewish charitable fundraising. For many Jews, activity in Jewish fundraising, in its turn, led to activity in non-Jewish (general community) fundraising.

The most recent NJPS of 2000–01 supported the earlier findings of increased Jewish charitable giving linked to age, income, institutional affiliations, and region of the country. Some of the Jewish normative factors were also associated with giving to and activities in non-Jewish charities. Overall, more education, family income, activity in Jewish community voluntary associations, and contributions to Jewish charities had moderate impacts upon contributions to non-Jewish (general community) charities.

There was a small group of Jews who were not involved with their organized Jewish communities, but education and family income propelled them to make contributions to general community fundraising. Finally, the second model of giving to non-Jewish charities only accounted for about half of the overall model variance compared to the first model of giving to Jewish causes.

Note:
   1. See Jones (2006) for an analysis of giving and volunteering as alternative forms of "civic engagement."

Chapter Four

The Three Faces of Giving:
Donors, Affiliated, and Unaffiliated[1]

While Julius Caesar wrote that the physical world of Gaul may be divided into three parts, the rabbis wrote that the spiritual world may also be divided into three. For example in the classical rabbinic text of *Pirkei Avot (Sayings of the Sages 1:2)*, it is written that the world rests on three pillars: *torah* (study), *avodah* (religious service), and *gmilut hasadim* (acts of loving kindness). Similarly, the author of Corinthians I in the New Testament, whose life coincided with that of some of the rabbis, taught in threes, as in "faith, hope, and charity." Likewise, social scientists studying the empirical world of American Jewry might make a tri-partite distinction. Indeed, in studying the relationship of American Jews to giving to the UJA, it was suggested in the previous chapter that such giving is related to a pattern of identification and affiliation with the Jewish community. Hence, it was decided to study three comparison groups in regard to their relationship to giving to the UJA[2] (one of the predecessor organizations to UJC as noted earlier) or through their local Jewish federated community campaign:

1. ***Donors***: givers to UJA (preferably $500 or more) and synagogue members and/or members of two or more Jewish organizations.
2. ***Affiliated***: non-givers to UJA but synagogue members and/or members of two or more Jewish organizations (i.e., an intermediate group that is "affiliated organizationally" but "under-affiliated" from the point of view of UJA, to which they do not contribute); and
3. ***Unaffiliated***: non-givers to UJA and non-members of a synagogue or two or more Jewish organizations.

Interviews were carried out in the 1980s primarily with individuals who were: a. approximately between thirty-five to fifty years of age; b. native-born of native-born parents; and c. possessing a B.A. degree. The *Donors* group represented the Jewish community's "good givers."

57

The *Unaffiliated* represented a group uninvolved—perhaps unreachable according to some. Finally, the *Affiliated* share with the *Donors* the characteristic of Jewish organizational membership and would, therefore, be expected to give to the UJA but do not. It is the objective of the research presented in this chapter, which is based on a purposive sample of seventy-two cases[3] (twenty-four in each of the three groups) as noted in Chapter Two, to explore why the more marginal groups of Jews do not give. From the National Jewish Population Survey (NJPS) of 1990, it is known that the group claiming to have given to the UJA represented slightly less than one-half of the total adult Jewish population (45 percent). Those not giving to the UJA (see the "*Unaffiliated*" and "*Affiliated*" columns in Table 4.1) included those who were indifferent, hostile, or ignorant about the UJA despite the fact that a portion of this group was involved in the organizational life of the Jewish community.

Nevertheless, further analysis of NJPS suggested that those interviewed (generally young, third generation, and college graduates) represented only a very small proportion of American Jews. Why then should a study aimed at understanding the barriers and incentives to giving to the UJA focus on such a small element of the population? Of course, this small group is the source of the future generation's leadership with respect to charitable giving, and understanding them is crucial to understanding the future of giving in the larger community and society. It is important, however, to reiterate that *these seventy-two cases were not a representative sample of any sector of American Jewry*. The percentages presented, therefore, apply only to the seventy-two cases and not to any larger group. Thus, the *findings constitute the basis for plausible hypotheses to be subsequently tested on a representative sample of the American Jewish population*. The purpose of presenting these data for this small number is to locate these individuals in the larger mass of American Jewry and to offer some insights as to the direction future research might take.[4]

Biosocial Characteristics

Table 4.1 presents the effects of the biosocial characteristics (gender, age, and family life cycle) on membership in the three sample groups. While overall these cases contained more men (56 percent) than women (44 percent), as Table 4.1 shows, there is no proportional difference in the *gender composition* of each of the three groups. In other words, neither men nor women were more likely to be in the *Donors*, *Affiliated*, or *Unaffiliated* groups.[5] With regard to age, as Table 4.1 shows, older individuals (forty-five plus) were more likely to be *Donors* (44 percent) than younger individuals, and *Affiliated* were more concentrated in

Table 4.1 Affiliation Level by Biosocial Characteristics and Family Life Cycle

Biosocial

| | Gender (100%, n=72) | | Age (100%, n=71) | | |
	Male (56%, n=40)	Female (44%, n=32)	Under 40 (66%, n=47)	40-44 (21%, n=15)	45+ (13%, n=9)
Donors	32%	34%	31%	33%	44%
Affiliated	35%	31%	38%	26%	22%
Unaffiliated	32%	34%	30%	40%	33%
Total	99%*	99%*	99%*	99%*	99%*

Family Life Cycle

| | # of Children (100%, n=71) | | | # of Children at Home (100%, n=70) | | | Age of Children (100%, n=97) | | |
	0 (17%, n=12)	1 (24%, n=17)	2+ (59%, n=42)	0 (23%, n=16)	1 (26%, n=18)	2+ (51%, n=36)	5 or below (37%, n=36)	6-12 (37%, n=36)	13+ (26%, n=25)
Donors	25%	22%	42%	31%	22%	42%	33%	39%	52%
Affiliated	58%	22%	30%	50%	22%	30%	30%	33%	16%
Unaffiliated	17%	55%	28%	19%	55%	28%	36%	28%	32%
Total	100%	99%*	100%	100%	99%*	100%	99%*	100%	100%

*Note: *Error due to rounding.*

the under forty group (38 percent). No meaningful patterns were found for the *Unaffiliated* except that they were slightly more likely to be found in the forty to forty-four age group.

With respect to *family life cycle*, several specific variables were examined. Since 86 percent were married, there was not enough variation to make meaningful comparisons as to the relationship between *marital status* and affiliation levels. Further, while only 4 percent were currently divorced, 20 percent of all cases reporting (n=56) were divorced at least once. Here again the number of *ever-divorced* persons in the sample was rather small, but it did suggest a relationship between not being divorced and greater affiliation. Individuals who were never divorced were much more likely (33 percent) to be in the *Donors* group than those who were ever-divorced (9 percent). Looking at the effect of the *number of children* on affiliation level, as Table 4.1 shows, those individuals with two children or more were more likely (38 percent) than those with fewer children (25 percent or 23 percent) to be among the *Donors*. A similar situation prevailed when looking at the variable number of *children at home as observed in Table 4.1.* Those with two or more children at home were more likely to be among the donors (42 percent) compared to those with one child at home (22 percent). Those with no children at home had 31 percent in the *Donor* group. Table 4.1 revealed that those with the oldest children were more likely to be the *Donors* (52 percent) compared to those with children six to twelve (39 percent) and those with children under six (33 percent). *These findings with regard to biosocial characteristics for this small number of cases were similar to that of the much larger NJPS sample.*

Socioeconomic Characteristics

Table 4.2 presents the effects of socioeconomic characteristics (formal education, occupational rank, employment status, and income) on membership in the three sample groups. Since this purposive sample was chosen with the emphasis on the college educated, it is not surprising to learn that three-quarters of the overall sample (74 percent) had advanced degrees. With respect to *formal education*, those individuals who had advanced degrees were disproportionately in the *Donors* group (M.A., 40 percent; doctorate, 39 percent) compared to those with a B.A. degree (16 percent). The effect of education on membership in the *Affiliated* and *Unaffiliated* groups was in the opposite direction. Those with a B.A. were disproportionately in the *Unaffiliated* group (44 percent), compared to those with a doctorate (26 percent). Thus, the higher the level of formal education achieved, the greater the likelihood of being a donor and making

Table 4.2 Affiliation Level by Socioeconomic Characteristics

	Formal Education (99%*, n=71)			Occupational Rank (100%, n=65)		
	BA (25%, n=18)	MA (42%, n=30)	Doctorate (32%, n=23)	Major Professionals and Higher Executives (43%, n=28)	Managers and Lesser Professionals (26%, n=17)	Sales, Clerical, Manual, etc. (31%, n=20)
Donors	16%	40%	39%	36%	23%	45%
Affiliated	39%	27%	35%	36%	35%	25%
Unaffiliated	44%	33%	25%	28%	41%	30%
Total	99%*	100%	99%*	100%	99%*	100%

	Employment Status (100%, n=60)		Income (100%, n=62)		
	Self-Employed (40%, n=24)	Not Self-Employed (60%, n=36)	0-$29,999 (23%, n=14)	$30,000-$74,999 (34%, n=21)	$75,000+ (43%, n=27)
Donors	42%	25%	28%	19%	59%
Affiliated	29%	28%	21%	33%	30%
Unaffiliated	29%	47%	50%	48%	11%
Total	100%	100%	99%*	100%	100%

*Note: * Error due to rounding.*

contributions to UJA for the group studied. This is likely to be so because many highly educated professionals (e.g., doctors and lawyers) have practices tied to their ethnic community and/or higher incomes necessary for extensive involvement in the community. (Other highly educated professionals, e.g., academicians and scientists are likely to be more integrated into their work community than their ethnic community because they are employed in a bureaucratic organization and are more geographically mobile.)

With respect to *occupational rank* as seen in Table 4.2, the respondents (n=65) reflected their high educational attainments with 43 percent of all respondents in the highest ranking occupations (major professionals and executives), 26 percent in the next highest category (managers and lesser professionals), and 31 percent in the remaining categories (sales, clerical, and manual). High-ranking occupations (major professionals and higher executives) seemed to predispose individuals to be more likely to be among the *Donors* (36 percent) than were managers and lesser professionals (23 percent), but both were exceeded in the *Donors* category by sales, clerical, and manual employees (45 percent). How can this apparent contradiction be explained? The question may be addressed by examining the next variable, *self-employment*. Those individuals who were self-employed were more likely to be among the *Donors* (42 percent) than those not self-employed (25 percent). For the *Affiliated*, there was virtually no difference, and those not self-employed were more likely to be in the *Unaffiliated* group (47 percent) than those self-employed (29 percent). What these findings suggest is that for this sample, formal education was more likely associated with affiliation if the formal education led to a self-employed occupation (e.g., doctor, lawyer, business person). Likewise, the sales, clerical, and manual employees may have also been disproportionately self-employed.

Furthermore, those self-employed were likely to have higher incomes than salaried employees and more likely to be *Affiliated*. Table 4.2 looks at *income* and shows individuals with higher incomes (of $75,000 or more in the 1980s) were disproportionately in the *Donors* group (59 percent) compared to those earning less than $30,000 (28 percent) or $30,000–$74,999 (19 percent). By contrast, those with incomes of less than $30,000 were much more likely to be *Unaffiliated* (50 percent) than those with incomes $75,000 and above (11 percent). The findings with respect to self-employment for this small group were similar to that of the much larger NJPS sample. *This finding is very complementary to that of Winter (1985), who documented the high cost of living a Jewish life, and Dashefsky and Shapiro (1974), who found that income had a positive independent effect on Jewish identification.*

Jewish Socialization

Evidence was offered in an earlier chapter that Jewish charitable giving was associated with Jewish affiliation and identification. This finding was supported by Cohen (1979), based on data gathered in the Boston study sponsored by the Combined Jewish Philanthropies, in which he found an increasing impact from 1965 to 1975 of Jewish activities on charitable giving as reported in Chapter Two.

Table 4.3 shows that the number of *Years of Jewish Education* was associated with being a *Donor*. Individuals with ten or more years of Jewish education were *more likely* to be *Donors* (44 percent) than those with five or fewer years of education. Conversely those individuals with the lowest level of Jewish education were much more likely to be among the *Unaffiliated* (38 percent) than those with ten or more years of education (11 percent).

Table 4.3 also looks at *Intensiveness of Jewish Education* and reveals that individuals with less intensive Jewish education were more than twice as likely to be in the *Unaffiliated* group (33 percent) than those with more intensive Jewish education (15 percent). For the *Affiliated*, the pattern was the reverse, and for the *Donors*, no real differences existed. The latter finding on the absence of an effect of intensiveness of Jewish education on being among the *Donors* suggests that length of time in the system (years of Jewish education) may trump intensiveness for this very small sub-sample (n=13).

In addition, Table 4.3 permits an assessment of the effects of *Adult Jewish Education* on UJA contribution. Those individuals who had exposure to some adult Jewish educational programs were more likely to be among the *Donors* (39 percent) than those who had none (22 percent). The pattern was the reverse among the *Affiliated*, with individuals who had no such exposure more likely to be in that group (52 percent) than those who had some adult Jewish education (25 percent). In the case of the *Unaffiliated*, individuals with some exposure to adult Jewish education were slightly more likely to be in that group than those who had none. Interestingly enough, the *Unaffiliated* resembled more the *Donors* on this variable. Perhaps, their exposure to some adult Jewish education suggests that these individuals were not wholly indifferent to Jewish life but to certain more "establishment" forms of Jewish life, such as UJA affiliation and contribution. *In sum, the findings with respect to Jewish education for this small number of cases were largely similar to the results of the much larger NJPS sample.*

Another dimension of Jewish education is contained in the informal approach of youth group and summer camp experiences, whose direct effects on

Table 4.3 Affiliation Level by Jewish Education Socialization Experiences

	Years of Jewish Education (100%, n=61)			Intensiveness of Jewish Education (100%, n=58)	
	0-5 (55%, n=34)	6-9 (32%, n=18)	10+ (13%, n=9)	Elementary or Sunday/Afternoon School (76%, n=45)	Elementary Day School or any and Above High School (24%, n=13)
Donors	29%	33%	44%	36%	38%
Affiliated	32%	33%	44%	31%	46%
Unaffiliated	38%	33%	11%	33%	15%
Total	99%*	99%*	99%*	100%	99%*

	Adult Jewish Education (100%, n=71)		Membership in Jewish Youth Groups (100%, n=50)		Jewish Camp Experience (100%, n=72)	
	No (32%, n=23)	Yes (68%, n=48)	No (55%, n=27)	Yes (45%, n=23)	No (64%, n=46)	Yes (36%, n=26)
Donors	22%	39%	30%	26%	35%	31%
Affiliated	52%	25%	22%	35%	37%	27%
Unaffiliated	26%	35%	48%	39%	28%	42%
Total	100%*	99%*	100%	100%	100%	100%

*Note: * Error due to rounding.*

Jewish identification have not been as clearly documented as formal Jewish education. Table 4.3 permits an examination of the influence of participation in *Jewish youth groups*. No clear-cut effects were observed. Those who had some youth group experience were more likely to be among the *Affiliated* than those who had none. For the *Unaffiliated*, those who had no such experiences were more likely to be in that group than those who had some. Such informal educational experiences did not appear as reliable predictors of affiliation as formal education for this small sample.

The data also failed to reveal any apparent pattern of influence linking an experience with *Jewish camping* to affiliation as shown in Table 4.3. Of course, most individuals in the sample (64 percent) had no such experience. Indeed, those who had reported some Jewish educational camp experience were more likely to be among the *Unaffiliated* (42 percent) than those reporting no camping experience (28 percent). Perhaps such an experience, a generation or more ago, turned individuals off to "establishment Jewish organizations," such as the UJA or Federation, but the data were not strong enough to warrant such a conclusion.

Dimensions of Denominational and Synagogue Involvement

Denominational Preference has been identified as an important variable in studying Jewish identification (see Lazerwitz, Winter, Dashefsky, and Tabory 1998; Harrison and Lazerwitz 1982; Lazerwitz and Harrison 1979; Lazerwitz 1979 and 1978). In Table 4.4, the data revealed that persons who preferred the Orthodox and Conservative denominations (50 percent and 48 percent respectively) were twice more likely to be among the *Donors* than those who preferred Reform (24 percent) and "other" or "no preference" (21 percent). Among the *Affiliated*, those who preferred Reform were more likely to be represented there (52 percent) than those who preferred the Conservative denomination (37 percent). Finally, those who chose "other/none" as their preference were much more likely to be among the *Unaffiliated* (79 percent) than those who chose Reform (24 percent) or Conservative (15 percent). The Orthodox cases were too few to discuss with only four cases reporting that denomination. Clearly, a more traditional denominational preference was associated with being affiliated with the UJA campaign. Nevertheless, of the nineteen cases (79 percent) among the *Unaffiliated* preferring other or none, we know from the raw data that most chose "other," again indicating that those individuals were not wholly psychologically isolated from Jewish identification. Indeed, out of the twenty-four cases among the *Unaffiliated*, only six (25 percent) chose no denominational preference suggesting that most of the individuals had some level of Jewish identification even though it was more symbolic.

Table 4.4 Affiliation Level by Denominational Preference, Membership and Synagogue Attendance

	Denominational Preference (100%, n=71)				Denominational Membership (100%, n=70)			
	Orthodox (5%, n=4)	Conservative (38%, n=27)	Reform (30%, n=21)	Other/ None (27%, n=19)	Orthodox (11%, n=8)	Conservative (29%, n=20)	Reform (16%, n=11)	Other/None (44%, n=31)
Donors	50%	48%	24%	21%	50%	55%	27%	19%
Affiliated	50%	37%	52%	0%	50%	45%	73%	3%
Unaffiliated	0%	15%	24%	79%	0%	0%	0%	77%
Total	100%	100%	100%	100%	100%	100%	100%	99%*

	Synagogue Attendance (100%, n=71)		
	Frequent: Weekly to Monthly (30%, n=21)	Intermediate: Monthly and less (58%, n=41)	None (12%, n=9)
Donors	52%	29%	0%
Affiliated	43%	36%	0%
Unaffiliated	5%	34%	100%
Total	100%	99%*	100%

*Note: *Error due to rounding.*

Table 4.4 on *Denominational Membership* produced somewhat similar findings. Individuals who belonged to an Orthodox or Conservative synagogue were more likely (50 percent and 55 percent respectively) to be among the *Donors* than those who belonged to a Reform temple (27 percent) or who had no congregational affiliation (19 percent). Conversely members of a Reform temple were more likely to be among the *Affiliated* (73 percent) than those who belonged to a Conservative congregation (45 percent). The number of individuals belonging to Orthodox synagogues in the sample was rather small (n=8 or 11 percent), but the direction of the findings was similar to the Conservative members. Of course, all of the individuals among the *Unaffiliated* did not belong to a synagogue as previously specified. Therefore, no comparison is possible. In sum, membership in a more traditional synagogue (Orthodox or Conservative) was associated with a greater likelihood of being affiliated with the UJA campaign.

With respect to *Synagogue Attendance*, a similar pattern prevailed. Table 4.4 revealed that those individuals who attended more frequently (monthly or more) were more likely to be among the *Donors* (52 percent) than those who attended less than once a month, usually on the High Holidays (29 percent). No great difference was observed among the *Affiliated*. However, individuals who *never* attended synagogue were much more likely to be in the *Unaffiliated* group (100 percent) than those who attended less than monthly (34 percent). Because almost all of the individuals among the *Donors* or *Affiliated* belonged to a synagogue, no one reported not attending synagogue at all. Likewise, only one individual among the *Unaffiliated* reported frequent synagogue attendance. Here again the pattern is repeated with a higher level of synagogue attendance associated with a greater likelihood of being among the *Donors* and *Affiliated* groups. *Again, the findings for synagogue attendance for this small number of cases were similar to that of the larger NJPS sample.*

Organizational Involvement

Table 4.5 also examined the effects of organizational and friendship involvements on affiliation with UJA. Table 4.5 showed that those individuals who were members of four or more Jewish organizations or clubs were more likely to be among the *Donors* (67 percent) than those who belonged to fewer (26 percent) or those who were non-members (24 percent). (Of course, those who were among the *Affiliated* were selected only if they were non-members or at the most had one membership.)

Table 4.5 also allowed for an examination of the effects of the level of *Jew-*

ish Organizational Involvement on affiliation, but no significant differences were observed. Individuals who were more actively involved were only slightly more likely to be in the *Affiliated* group (50 percent) than those who were occasionally involved (39 percent). Perhaps such involvement lowered their interest in or financial commitment to UJA. As expected, the small number of cases of organizational involvement occurring among the *Unaffiliated* was self-evident by the definition of the category.

What about the effects of involvement in general clubs? Here Table 4.5 showed that the pattern was similar to Jewish organizational membership. Those individuals who had four or more *General Organizational Memberships* were more likely to be among the *Donors* (43 percent) than those with some memberships (30 percent) or no membership (16 percent). By contrast, those with no memberships were more likely to be among the *Unaffiliated* (42 percent) than those who belonged to many such clubs (27 percent). The pattern for the *Affiliated* was somewhat similar to the *Unaffiliated*. This suggests that *General Organizational Membership* as well as *Jewish Organizational Memberships* were positively associated with UJA affiliation. *Thus, the mere fact of having multiple organizational memberships appeared to make individuals more likely—and not less likely—to take on another affiliation or involvement, such as a commitment to UJA.*

Finally, Table 4.5 permitted an examination of the effect of informal Jewish friendship association (*Proportion of Friends Jewish*) on affiliation. The findings were similar to that for formal *Jewish Organizational Involvement*. Those individuals who reported that less than half their close friends were Jewish were much more likely to be among the *Unaffiliated* (75 percent) than those who reported about half (40 percent) or nearly all (16 percent) of their friends were Jewish. By contrast those who reported all or nearly all their friends were Jewish were more likely to be among the *Donors* (42 percent) than those who reported about half (35 percent) or less than half (0 percent) of their friends were Jewish. The *Affiliated* were more similar in this regard to the *Donors*.

Summary

The quantitative evidence presented in Chapter Three is supplemented beginning in Chapter Four with the results of qualitative interviews, an approach consistent with that of Fishman, who noted the following:

> Survey research is of critical importance in helping us see the big picture. However, although such statistical research excels in determining the broad meters of behavior, it is not a refined enough instrument for understanding why

Table 4.5 Affiliation Level by Organizational and Friendship Involvements

	No. of Jewish Organizational Memberships (99%*, n=71)			Jewish Organizational Involvement (100%, n=45)	
	0 (30%, n=21)	Some: 1-3 (49%, n=35)	Many: 4+ (20%, n=15)	Occasional (51%, n=23)	Active (49%, n=22)
Donors	24%	26%	67%	39%	36%
Affiliated	24%	37%	33%	39%	50%
Unaffiliated	52%	37%	0%	22%	14%
Total	100%	100%	100%	100%	100%

	No. of General Organizational Memberships (99%*, n=72)			Proportion of Friends Jewish (100%, n=70)		
	0 (17%, n=12)	Some: 1-3 (41%, n=30)	Many: 4+ (41%, n=30)	Less than Half (17%, n=12)	Half and More (29%, n=20)	All or Nearly All (54%, n=38)
Donors	16%	30%	43%	0%	35%	42%
Affiliated	42%	33%	30%	25%	25%	42%
Unaffiliated	42%	37%	27%	75%	40%	16%
Total	100%	100%	100%	100%	100%	99%*

*Note: *Error due to rounding.*

> people and societies behave as they do, or what might influence their future at-
> titudes and behaviors. Qualitative research . . . based on systematic personal in-
> terviews . . . provides effective techniques for looking at specific, targeted types
> of individuals and societies. When designing qualitative research projects, re-
> searchers characteristically search for representative paradigms rather than for
> huge numbers of informants (Fishman 2001:1).

Thus, the findings in this small sample with respect to Jewish and general organizational involvement were similar to the findings of the larger NJPS sample;
namely, greater organizational involvement was associated with a greater likelihood of being a donor. In regard to family life cycle, those with two children
were more likely to be donors. Similarly, the variable of self-employment was
more associated with being a donor. In addition, the findings with respect to
Jewish education and synagogue attendance revealed that more Jewish education and more frequent synagogue attendance were linked to a greater likelihood
of being donors. While the seventy-two cases did not constitute a probability
sample, the relationship between their general and Jewish background characteristics and their affiliation with UJA, or lack of it, was fairly consistent with the
national picture obtained from a larger NJPS sample. These findings further
substantiate the usefulness of linking both quantitative and qualitative data sets
to further understand the dynamics of charitable giving.

The *Affiliated* and *Unaffiliated* may give in the future. Even Bill Gates of
Microsoft appeared to come late to making charitable donations as reported by
Moran (1999) on the entrepreneur's $5 billion gift to the William H. Gates
Foundation or for that matter Steven Spielberg and his generous contributions to
the Shoah Foundation. Perhaps it takes role models at each level of giving to
stimulate further philanthropy among peers as well as motivation through the
life cycle to be concerned with a legacy for posterity. Consider Warren Buffet's
recent generosity in bequeathing $31 billion, most of his fortune, to the Gates
Foundation.

The data presented were illustrative of the characteristics of those interviewed and helped to locate the individuals in the larger American Jewish community. The findings reported in this chapter have set the stage for a discussion
of the thematic concerns of this book for the three groups (*Donors*, *Affiliated*,
and *Unaffiliated*) in the succeeding chapters.

Notes:
    1. Parts of this chapter were adapted from Dashefsky and Lazerwitz (1983).
Special thanks are owed to Sam Richardson, graduate assistant in the Berman

Institute—North American Jewish Data Bank for assistance in reformatting the tables in this chapter.

2. Throughout this chapter and the succeeding chapters, we will use the term UJA (United Jewish Appeal), the predecessor organization to UJC or United Jewish Communities, for that is how respondents referred to it as a proxy for the local Jewish federation.

3. The sample included interviews in four urbanized regions of the United States: Florida, New England, New York, and Texas. The interview schedule underwent a series of several different versions, five in all, which were developed during the period from November 1981 until March 1982. The great majority of the interviews, those from New York and New England, were gathered using Version 5 of the schedule; the others utilized the slightly different Version 4. A small group of individuals were interviewed using Version 6 for a focus group approach, in which the closed-ended questions were filled out in a questionnaire and the open-ended questions were asked in the interview.

4. Despite the span of time between gathering of these data in the 1980s and the present time, subsequent interviews carried out at the dawn of the twenty-first century with professionals involved in the Jewish federation movement confirmed most of the findings as noted in Chapter Seven.

5. The findings presented in the tables in this chapter in some cases yield small cell sizes. Nevertheless, the findings reported are consistent with those cited in Chapter Three, which were derived from large sample surveys. Therefore, the evidence offered in this chapter and the succeeding Chapters Five and Six provide more detail than is possible in large scale sample surveys, all of which enrich the understanding and explanation for charitable choices and the motivations for such giving.

Chapter Five

Group Portraits in Three Dimensions: Comparisons and Contrasts[1]

Bernie Marcus was just a young boy the first time he donated nickels to help plant trees in Israel. "That's what my mother taught me, that you have to give back," says the seventy-four-year-old cofounder and retired CEO of The Home Depot. "In fact, I couldn't understand why I was doing it. This was my ice cream money that I was giving away. But she said, 'You have to help people who are less fortunate; this is what we do.' It's called *tzedakah* in Hebrew" (Wurst 2003:42).

Bernie Marcus's mother knew that traditional Jewish religion had set forth specific standards and expectations for its followers (as noted in Chapter Two) and she wanted to be certain her son understood this as well. To be sure, Judaism provides a wealth of information on the norms governing Jewish charitable behavior, *tzedakah*, as found in the Tanakh, the Talmud, and the Midrash. Indeed, in years past, *tzedakah* was well-integrated into the daily life of the Jews, and institutions were developed to provide for the social and welfare needs of the community, harking back to the Middle Ages and earlier. *Tzedakah* was expected from all Jews—even the poor—according to Maimonides, the renowned medieval Jewish philosopher.

Indeed, Maimonides saw in charitable giving the formation of community in a series of concentric circles. "A poor person who is your relative should receive your charity before all others; and likewise the poor of your own household have priority over the poor of your city; and the poor of your city have priority over the poor of another city, as it is stated in the Torah, 'To poor and needy brothers in your land'" (Deuteronomy 15:11) (Maimonides, Mishneh Torah, Laws of Tzedakah 7:13 as cited in Isaacs 2005:27). Nevertheless, Maimonides recognized the obligation of the Jewish community to the non-Jewish poor. He wrote, "One is required to feed and clothe the non-Jewish poor together with the poor of Israel, this for the sake of peace" (Maimonides, Mishneh Torah, Laws of Tzedakah 7:17 as cited in Isaacs 2005:26).

While these traditional messages and meanings of *tzedakah* may appeal to the *Donors*, do they say anything to the *Affiliated* and the *Unaffiliated*? Perhaps, the best way to address this question is to take some prototypical examples from within each of the three groups (*Donors*, *Affiliated*, and *Unaffiliated*), described in the previous chapter, and offer a portrait of each.

Portraits of the Donors

The minimum criteria of membership in the group of *Donors* were contributing to the UJA (preferably $500 or more) and membership in a synagogue and/or two or more Jewish organizations. Consider the case of Ms. S. At the time of the interview, she was thirty-five years old, married, with two school-age children. While she was raised in a small Jewish community in upstate New York, she had lived in southern New England for twelve years, currently in a town identified as having the largest number of Jews in the metropolitan area. Having earned an M.A. degree, she was working part-time away from home. While Ms. S. grew up in a Conservative Jewish home, she considered herself Reform and belonged to a Reform temple. She had an average amount of Jewish education, attending five years of Sunday and Hebrew school.

In the case of Ms. S., the key to her commitment to UJA, she believed, stemmed from her childhood socialization, in particular, discussions at the dinner table. While only her grandfather was born abroad, the fact that HIAS (Hebrew Immigrant Aid Society) helped him upon his arrival at Ellis Island was very important to her. Since she mentioned it twice in the interview, it appeared likely to be significant in understanding her commitment to UJA. This same grandfather helped organize the first Conservative synagogue in her hometown, and her father was president of the local Jewish Community Center. Ms. S. came with Jewish socialization experiences rooted in activity and commitment to organized Jewish life. As she said, "It's family tradition that has a lot to do with it." In fact, she and her husband spent their honeymoon in Israel—for six weeks. Ms. S. believed, however, that her family did not contribute enough to the local campaign although they gave $5,000 over each of the past two years based on a family salary in six digits. She alone decided how much to give. Ms. S. was, perhaps, the epitome of the Federation executive's dream of a Young Leader. Her involvement stemmed from her socialization in a family committed to Jewish community involvement and her level of giving was a function of her very high family income.

Consider the case of Mr. K. He was forty-one years old at the time of the interview and married, with three school-age children. While he grew up in Brooklyn, he was living in Long Island, working as a CPA and self-employed.

He considered himself to be a Conservative Jew and was a member of a Conservative congregation, where he attended services several times a month. He had a typical Jewish education through Bar Mitzvah, attending school on Sundays and afternoons. While he was not highly involved in Jewish organizations, he suggested that 80–90 percent of his close friends were Jewish. As he put it, "I have to have my people around me."

In discussing the reasons for his being committed to the local campaign, to which he gave over $500 on a more than moderate salary, Mr. K. stated:

> If you were looking at what made me a contributor, I would say that . . . my father didn't have a lot of money; but it was his nature that if someone put their hand out and they needed, he may not have had, but they got. And it doesn't have to be verbalized that some people are givers, and others are takers. If there had to be any distinction between givers and non-givers, it would be to see what the parents did.

Then there was the case of Ms. C. She was thirty-one years old at the time of the interview, married with one pre-school child and expecting another. While she grew up in a small town in the northwestern United States, she was living in a large metropolitan area in Texas. Ms. C. had a master's degree and was trained as a psychiatric social worker, but she has been working primarily as a homemaker. She considered herself Conservative but belonged to an Orthodox congregation and attended services several times a month. In the Jewish community of her youth, she had a Sunday school Jewish education, which lasted for nine years (more than the norm) and was planning to send her children to a day school. Ms. C. belonged to a variety of local Jewish organizations, including the Community Center and Hadassah and held leadership positions. She was also a member of several general community organizations. Finally, her close friends were nearly all Jewish. Ms. C.'s family gift to the local campaign was over $2,500 on a more than moderate income. She was deeply committed to Jewish life as well as to personal practice in the home. The origins of her commitment to Jewish life and the UJA were rooted in her family experiences. She was very close to her grandparents, who escaped from Nazi Germany. Ms. C. recounted her grandparents' flight from Germany:

> They were in Germany; and they were very, very wealthy people. They had a big store, and they lived behind the store, and this was before Kristallnacht [the "night of shattered glass" when Nazi pogroms against Jews and their property and synagogues were carried out in Germany in the night of November 9–10, 1938]. One morning she woke up and found the store was totally defaced. And she had already lived through pogroms; and she [grandmother] said to my grandfather, "We are getting out." And he said, "Don't be silly. This can't happen here." That whole scene from the Holocaust. . . . He said, "Oh, that's silly.

It can't happen here. Don't believe it." And she said, "Fine, you stay; and I'm taking the children, and I'm going. And if you want to come, you can come; but I'm not going to stay here."

Ms. C. went on to explain her close ties to her small-town Jewish community and to her father, who died in middle-age:

I was brought up feeling very special because I was Jewish. Positively so! Oh yes, I mean being Jewish was very important to my family—not that Federation was part of my life—but my fondest memories were of sitting *in shul* [synagogue] playing with the strings of my father's *tallis* [prayer shawl]—just real positive memories.

But there were also negative experiences that shaped her Jewish identification:

My first was in first grade, and one of my closest friends called me a "dirty Jew." And I can close my eyes and tell you what we were both wearing. I'll never forget that. So I had experiences like that. Being Jewish was just a big part of my life.

What do these portraits have in common? They represent individuals who had Jewish socialization experiences rooted in the family and community involvement and/or giving of charity. At the time of the interviews, they were enmeshed in the Jewish community through organizational involvement, synagogue membership, and/or almost exclusively, a Jewish friendship network. Add to this that they all had substantial family incomes, which made it possible for them to implement the commitments they developed. As Cohen concluded: "Putting things crudely, it appears that deciding whether to give is a Jewish decision; deciding what to give is an economic one" (1979:50).

Portraits of the Unaffiliated

Attention now turns to the *Unaffiliated* group. They were selected because they were not contributors to the UJA campaign and nonmembers of a synagogue or two or more Jewish organizations. Some individuals did belong to one Jewish organization, such as a community center, Hadassah, or a Jewish fellowship group; but, in general, this group was very marginal to the organized Jewish community.

Take the case of Mr. G. He was thirty-seven years old at the time of the interview, a divorced father of one child, who spent part of the time with him. Mr. G. grew up in Cleveland and had lived in a metropolitan area of southern

New England for fourteen years. A college graduate, he worked as a research engineer for a corporation and earned a moderate salary.

Mr. G. had a Sunday school education as a child for five years with some mid-week instruction. He did not accept any conventional Jewish denominational preference such as Orthodox, Conservative or Reform. While Mr. G., of course, did not belong to a synagogue, he attended a Havurah group (an informal Jewish fellowship group) and religious services several times a year. Even though he did not belong to any other Jewish organizations, he did belong to several general professional and community associations. In addition, more than half of his friends were Jewish.

The best way to summarize Mr. G's. attitude (toward his lack of affiliation with UJA and his general low level of Jewish involvement) is to use his own statement about himself, "I am a child of the sixties." By that, he meant he had a distrust of anyone who told him he should do something: "If someone says, 'he should do this,' I say, 'I don't want to do this,' before I even know what *this* (italics for emphasis) is." And yet, this was misleading. It is more appropriate to say that he was aware of the need to give charity and did so, but not within the realm of the establishment. Evidence of this was found in his decision to stop giving to the United Fund. He did contribute to two causes which he sought out: a health charity and Amnesty International.

His Jewish identity also took an anti-establishment form in that he had joined a Havurah group, but he again showed self-motivation by attending the Jewish Awareness Seminar sponsored by the local Federation. He felt they were informative and was not "turned off" by going into the posh homes (a different one for each lecture) as some of those who attended had been, according to his report.

He had traveled to Israel and from this became more aware of its precarious "geography." And yet, he did not contribute to UJA. When asked if he could direct his dollars to a specific social program in Israel, he still resisted, saying that he preferred direct contributions. He enjoyed writing a check to a particular charity and knowing that every penny went directly there. He had a sense of giving only in that manner. This experience foreshadowed the emergent twenty-first century trend of entrepreneurial giving reported by the Federation directors in Chapter Seven. He also disliked solicitation of all kinds and spoke in terms of time wasted by such activity.

Mr. and Ms. N. are two other members of the *Unaffiliated* group. He was forty-four at the time of the interview, and she was forty. They had two school-aged children. While Mr. N. has lived all his life in New York City, Ms. N. was raised in a metropolitan area of upstate New York and had lived in the city for the past eighteen years. He earned a doctorate and worked for the Board of Education; she, a college graduate, was self-employed in crafts. Their family income was moderate.

Ms. N. had no Jewish education and Mr. N. attended a community after-noon school for three years. They did not accept any conventional Jewish deno-minational preference. They thought of themselves as "ethnically Jewish" and did not attend religious services at all during the twelve months preceding the interview. They did, however, belong to the local Jewish Y and were members of several professional and community associations. Most of their friends were intermarried and so they estimated that only half their friends were Jewish. Fi-nally, in regard to their Jewish identification they believed that the Jewish edu-cation of their children was the children's own choice.

This is how they responded to the question:

Interviewer (I): Which kind of Jewish education is, was or will be given [to] your children?
Mr. N.: Not now they're not (receiving any).
I: Did they ever. . . ?
Mr. N.: Well, it's their choice.
Ms. N.: Literally, their choice. . . . She (daughter) doesn't lean towards it. She doesn't want to.
Mr. N.: As a matter of fact, she's made her decision.
Ms. N.: She goes back and forth. There was a time when she would go to Tem-ple with her friends and then (was) turned off again. Right now, she's off.
Mr. N.: She's been off for quite a while, and she's made her decisions by say-ing she doesn't believe.
Ms. N.: Yeh.
Mr. N.: That's what I mean by that.
Ms. N.: But she's changeable, and she's going into puberty and adolescence; and a lot of her opinions are going to change back and forth for the next few years.
I: And everything is up for grabs as far as your son goes?
Ms. N.: Right, now, nothing. I guess we'll kind of wait and see what he decides later.
I: Do you think he'll want to be Bar Mitzvahed?
Ms. N.: He (the son) will probably say no.
Mr. N.: I will say no. . . .
Ms. N.: I would see what he'd want to do.

The best way to summarize Mr. and Ms. N.'s virtual lack of Jewish affiliation and involvement is their lack of Jewish socialization and Mr. N.'s political in-volvement. As he put it:

Mr. N.: I was extremely political by the time I was ten years old. I was politi-cized.
I: By whom?

Mr. N.: My grandfather was an old time socialist—an old time radical socialist, and I was very close with him. What happened was that he . . . my father and his brothers disagreed with him in his being unrealistic, etc., and so forth; and I didn't particularly like what they were saying; and I let them have it with both barrels; and I've been doing it ever since; and my grandfather likes to take them on; and so I evened up the sides a little. That's what really happened.

Nevertheless, Mr. N. has some measure of Jewish identification. When asked what type of activity outside the synagogue UJA could sponsor, he replied:

Mr. N.: I'll tell you something. Personally, if they had something like I went to those *folkshuls* [non-denominational communal schools which emphasized Yiddish as part of the curriculum], those cultural programs . . . I'd encourage my own kids to go. Whether they would or not is another story. We often try to find something like that. . . .
I: You like things in Yiddish?
Mr. N.: I think the Yiddish culture in some ways is far richer. . . . It's a secular sense to it that [I like] . . . what I call the Jewish experience, and a sense of historical perspective, their background; and that's something I would like my own children to have, although they don't. It's always impossible to find such a thing around.

Moreover, when the N.'s were interested in disposing of some used clothing, they decided to donate it to a *Jewish* thrift shop and training center. In their minds, giving money was not as important as being involved—especially politically.

Mr. N.: No. I'll tell you something about that. For me, I have to speak for myself. If I have been involved in something, I feel a hell of a lot better than when I've given anything. It's almost meaningless to me to give some money to a cause. I don't have an emotional response; but if I have actively participated in some way in some cause, that has meaning.
I: Can you think of any such instances that were particularly meaningful to you?
Mr. N.: Yeh, I can give a number. When I was involved in the ban the bomb movement in the early 1960s. That was before we were married. And I was in Washington when Kennedy made the big speech.
I: Was there any financial contribution involved along with participation. Or just participation?
Mr. N.: It was just participation. I was active, doing. . . . That I found very satisfying—even now when I've been able to help get something done, even in the neighborhood. . . .

Another example of the *Unaffiliated* type of person was Mr. L. He was thirty-nine years old at the time of this interview, married a second time and living with Ms. L's high school age daughter. Mr. L. was raised in Brooklyn, New York, and had lived in his metropolitan South Florida community for seven years. He had a master's degree, worked in educational administration, and had a moderate family income.

Mr. L. had a somewhat typical Jewish education, attending afternoon school for about five years. He considered himself Reform; and, of course, as he was unaffiliated by definition, he did not belong to a synagogue nor to any Jewish organizations. Mr. L., however, indicated that he did attend religious services occasionally. While he did not belong to any Jewish organizations, he did belong to several (general community) professional, service, and recreational organizations and served as an officer in some civic organizations. Although Mr. L. reported that nearly all his friends were Jewish, his wife was not and his daughter received no Jewish education. The time of the interview was December, and in the living room, where the interview took place, was a large, decorated Christmas tree, and nearby was a Hanukkah menorah, occupying a much smaller presence.

According to Mr. L., his lack of involvement in the local UJA campaign was the result of his lack of funds. As he put it, "I've lived on a month-to-month basis." His lack of other Jewish commitments seemed to be rooted in his alienation from religion and synagogue life. As he explained it:

[Ms. L.] and I have both been married for a second time. When I first went to the Temple to inquire about marriage, I was handed a card asking for my occupation, my annual salary—exactly what my contributions should be based on—my earnings. It shook the foundations of my ideology and scared me away. And I didn't get married in that Temple.

Mr. L. seemed to be looking for non-synagogue types of Jewish cultural activity and even religious celebrations. When asked whether there were any activities outside of the synagogue that would interest him, he replied: "Something of a holiday nature would be very appealing. The fondest remembrance of childhood was the family holidays." Perhaps Mr. L.'s relationship to the Jewish community could be described as ambivalent. He had some fond childhood Jewish memories and would be interested in family-oriented Jewish activities outside the synagogue. Perhaps his ambivalence was best symbolized by the duality of their religious observance, represented by the Christmas tree and the Hanukkah menorah. Nevertheless, Mr. L. made a pledge to the local UJA campaign about the time of the interview.

What do these portraits have in common? They represent individuals who had very little Jewish socialization experiences in the family, community involvement, and the giving of charity. This led them to be less involved as adults in the formally organized Jewish community, to have far less informal friendship ties to Jews or more likely to have intermarried than was typical of the Donors. Nevertheless, they still claimed at least half their friends to be Jewish and did not disavow their Jewish identity. Finally, the income level reported was modest to moderate unlike the Affiliated group which had more than moderate to high incomes in the 1980s.

They were, moreover, responsive to pursuing tzedakah (in the sense of justice), such as the redemption of captives (as in the case of supporting Amnesty International) or the quest for peace (as in the "Ban the Bomb" movement). They may have even developed these concerns through their socialization in a highly secularized Jewish version of traditional tzedakah as justice, but they did not necessarily recognize it as such. Nor did the community seem to have a role for them to play consistent with their identities.

Thus, it seems that even among these Unaffiliated there remains "dos pintele yid," the jot of Jewishness, possessed with menshlikhkayt, a compassionate concern and sensitivity for others. The question remains whether these people can mobilize themselves or be mobilized by others to affirm their identities and activities as members of the Jewish community.

Portraits of Affiliated

In regard to the *Affiliated* group, it was defined as membership in a synagogue and/or two or more Jewish organizations but not having contributed to the UJA campaign. Thus, the *Affiliated* resembled the *Donors* by virtue of their synagogue (or Jewish organizational) membership, but they resembled the *Unaffiliated* in their not contributing to the campaign. Whom do they really most resemble?

Consider the situation of Mr. and Ms. O. At the time of the interview, he was thirty-six and she was thirty-three. They had three children, two in school and one pre-schooler. They both grew up in major northern metropolitan areas— he in New York and she in Chicago—and had lived for the past one and one-half years in a metropolitan South Florida community. They both attended college. He worked in real estate and she as a homemaker. They had a more than moderate income.

While Mr. O. grew up attending afternoon Hebrew school, studying Hebrew in the public high school, and belonging to Jewish youth groups, Ms. O. grew up as a Christian. She had, however, pursued a substantial amount of adult Jewish education courses, had a private tutor, and recently became a Bat Mitzvah. Now Mr. and Ms. O. consider themselves to be Reform and belong to a Reform congregation. They attended religious services on a weekly basis. While Mr. O. was a member of the Temple Brotherhood, Ms. O. was very active in several Jewish community organizations and had held a position as an officer. Moreover, they were both involved in general community organizations. Mr. O. was active in a humanitarian cause aimed at ending world hunger about which he spoke with great conviction and spiritual fervor. Ms. O. had been active in local school and political causes and they also belonged to a local country club.

While Mr. and Ms. O. were connected to Jewish organizational life—she, a convert, more than he—they did not give to the local campaign. Their Temple involvement gave them much pleasure, and they recently raised their contribution, increasing their charitable giving to over $2,500. Why did it give them so much satisfaction? Mr. O. explained:

> Because I'm there all the time, and I could see what is needed; so if I could see that we contributed to something they didn't have—I get pleasure out of seeing when I'm at services or whatever—or knowing that we've created a building. My highest amount of satisfaction is the money I give to the (humanitarian) project. I always experience reluctance in making contributions, yet I know that is what I want to do regardless of what I'm contributing to. I know that is what I really want to do, and the reluctance that I have is the comfortableness that I want to give as much as I sometimes do. I just feel that I'm philanthropic by nature, generally, and sometimes I am concerned whether I have the ability to give as much as I would like; so when I do give, it's very rewarding that I've made a commitment to do that. Once I've committed myself it's just a wonderful feeling and that's the way I feel with the contributions I've made to the (humanitarian) project; and I'll go on to say as far as the contributions we've made to our Temple, I feel equally rewarded that I have done that.

Why does their generosity and humanitarian concern not extend to the Federation/UJA Campaign?

> I would say for us and close friends, which we are talking about right now, I would say there is no feeling of Federation involvement in the community. ZERO! There is an awakening that is going on, but unfortunately, I don't know if it is too late. It's like "where were you when we needed you" type of attitude right now. It's a community of young people, who need the services, and they just didn't have the manpower, or they just didn't have something to be here in the past few years. There's a definite resentment about Federation. It comes from knowing *Federation here like sucks you in and drains you until you're dry* (italics for emphasis). So when you're interested in a few different things such as the Temple, different organizations, it's not okay to be just a small contributor to UJA—like [they want a] total commitment tie; I think people fear that. That needs to be overcome educationally.

Thus for the O.'s, the Temple is "there" providing "comfort," close friends, family activities, and a place for the children. While the Temple appeared psychologically close, the Federation appeared remote.

Another example of the *Affiliated* (who was a non-donor) was the case of Mr. R., forty years old and married for the second time with no children at the time of the interview. He grew up in New York City and continued to live there. Mr. R. went to law school and was in a private legal practice. His family income was more than moderate. As to his Jewish background, Mr. R. reported he had a very limited Jewish education lasting two or three years, and did not participate in any Jewish youth organizations. He thought of himself as culturally Jewish and belonged to a Reform temple, where he attended religious services several times a month. He was active in Jewish organizations, such as Bnai Brith, and served on the Board of Directors of his Temple. In addition, he was active in general fraternal and political organizations. Mr. R.'s wife was a convert to Judaism prior to their marriage and Mr. R. reported nearly all their friends to be Jewish.

Mr. R. was active and contributive to his Temple as well as other Jewish and general organizations, but he did not contribute to the local UJA Campaign. Why was he positively disposed to his synagogue and not to UJA? Mr. R. explained:

> The synagogue came to me in the time of my life when I needed to have a stronger Jewish identity. It provided that in a very warm, familiar atmosphere, something which was absent from most of my life (the warm, familiar atmosphere and, therefore, I felt very much at home). I did go to services and enjoyed them, and I became very involved. It was very familiar; that is the point. When a member of the family says they need some money, you say you will be happy. It's a very personal, direct contact kind of thing, and I know what the finances of the synagogue are . . . better than the average congregant because of my involvement on the board.

Not only was Mr. R. attracted to the Temple to support it, but he was repelled by UJA and its method of solicitation as he saw it:

> I can't set aside my personal offense at UJA methodology. I find it extraordinarily offensive. It's effective. It works. A lot of people give but not [me]. I really believe it to be offensive . . . standing up and saying how much people have given is an extraordinary, insensitive thing to do. But I think what one gives is between himself and their Maker and not a matter of public consumption. The fact that there are computer lists that indicate what I gave last year, the year before that, the year before that, and there is always this pressure to update it each year is extraordinarily offensive to me. I feel it's like a business. I don't owe UJA anything; and, therefore, I would find it extraordinarily offensive to have them call me up and say, "Hey, you gave this much last year," and it is done that way because I have been involved with it.

As Mr. R. explained later, he had been a solicitor for Israel Bonds which he felt used the same solicitation technique. *As with the O. 's, Mr. R. found his synagogue attractive because it offered him the psychological support he needed to express himself as a Jew. Whereas UJA offered none of this, Mr. R. found it repellent because of the solicitation techniques he perceived to be relying on public pledging. Moreover, his perceptions of UJA included that it was an impersonal, "computerized business," "high pressure," and also engendered "a feeling that no amount is really enough."* As he concluded, "I must feel that I have given to a *need,* not to a big organization."

Summary

While Chapter Four documented the parallels in charitable giving comparing the findings from national, quantitative studies to the qualitative interviews analyzed in this book, the current chapter delineated some of the differences in orientations that have emerged with respect to such charitable giving. The results of the analysis of the data obtained through in-depth interviews were presented as three separate portraits, defining the different orientations of the respondents to Jewish charitable giving and the reasons for it among the *Donors, Unaffiliated*, and *Affiliated*, described previously.

First, the *Donors* had Jewish socialization experiences rooted in the family and community involvement, and/or the giving of charity and were currently enmeshed in the community through organizational involvement, synagogue membership, and/or almost an exclusive Jewish friendship network along with more than moderate incomes. Second, the *Unaffiliated*, by contrast, consisted of individuals who had very little Jewish socialization experience in the family, community involvement, or the giving of charity. This led them to be less involved as adults in the formally organized Jewish community and to have far less informal Jewish friendship ties. They were more likely to be intermarried, even though they did not disavow their Jewish identification, and had only moderate incomes. Third, the *Affiliated* (with respect to the Jewish community but not UJA), resembled the *Donors*, in that they had Jewish roots and interconnections (e.g., synagogue membership and/or organizational involvement) but, like the *Unaffiliated*, did not give because they did not possess a positive image and personal understanding of what the UJA or the local Jewish Federation did even though many had more than moderate incomes.

While the *Affiliated* did not give to UJA, like the *Unaffiliated*, the former were largely different from the latter. The *Affiliated* had Jewish roots and interconnections like the *Donors*. What they lacked, compared to the *Donors*, was a positive image and personal understanding of what UJA does or how the local Jewish Federation served the Jewish Community. In part, this may have been the result of not being adequately informed as these individuals may be much newer to the community, or this may be the result of crude or negative solicitation techniques, or this may result from the lack of tangible needs that the UJA fulfilled for these people. What may be incentives as well as barriers to giving for these three groups will be examined in the next chapter.

Note:
1. Parts of this chapter were adapted with permission of the publisher from: Arnold Dashefsky. "Orientations Toward Jewish Charitable Giving." Pp. 19–34 in Nahum M.Waldman (ed.), *Community and Culture: Essays in Jewish Studies*. Philadelphia: Gratz College Seth-Press. Copyright © (1987) by Gratz College.

Chapter Six

Perceived Incentives and Barriers to Giving[1]

In a paper on "The Future of Jewish Giving in America," Ritterband and Cohen recounted the story first told by a Jew from Salonika (1979:1–2):

> The leadership of the Jewish community decided that it needed new medical facilities. To raise the money, a tax was levied on cheese. The Jewish grocers, fearful that the price increase caused by the cheese tax would decrease sales, refused to collect the tax. The rabbinic leadership in turn declared all their cheese to be non-kosher. Shortly thereafter, presumably with the decidedly unwelcome prospect of pound upon pound of rotting cheese on their hands, the grocers saw the justice of the cheese tax and agreed to collect the tax. Miraculously, the cheese became kosher again.

Those were the days! It certainly seemed easier to raise communal funds when there was a religious, legal system to support it. Of course, in American society, membership in the Jewish community and contributing to Jewish causes are voluntary acts. Why then do some Jews give? As Ritterband and Cohen go on to say, "Jews who take seriously one aspect of Jewish life tend to respond in like manner to other aspects including philanthropy" (1979:2). This observation is consistent with the findings which were reported earlier.

How do the three groups (the *Donors*, *Affiliated*, and *Unaffiliated*) perceive their relationship to the organized Jewish community with respect to contributing to the Federation or UJA? This chapter will examine what *they themselves* perceive as their incentives for and barriers to giving.

Comparisons Among the Three Groups

The *Donors* represented the Jewish community's "good givers." The *Affiliated* shared with the *Donors* the characteristic of Jewish organizational membership and would, therefore, be expected to give to UJA but did not. The *Unaffiliated* represented an uninvolved group, which, according to some, was unreachable.

In comparing the findings of this small sample to those reported for the

National Jewish Population Survey on a variety of social, economic, and reli-gious characteristics, the data revealed that those who had children, were self-employed, had more Jewish education, were frequent synagogue attendees, and had more Jewish and general organizational involvements were more likely to contribute to the UJA. Such evidence was consistent with that of other research-ers. For example, Cohen's study (1979), based on data gathered in Boston, found an increasing impact from 1965 to 1975 of Jewish activities on charitable giving. A study in Israel found that religious Israeli Jews were significantly more charitable than the secular Jews studied (Yinon and Sharon 1985).

While the individuals specially interviewed in this book were not statistical-ly representative of the entire American Jewish community, they were illustra-tive of the patterns of affiliation with UJA and Jewish organizational life—or the lack of it. How, then, did the three groups of individuals (*Donors*, *Affiliated*, and *Unaffiliated*) view their relationship to the organized Jewish community with respect to contributing to UJA? What did they perceive as incentives for and barriers to giving?

Table 6.1 summarizes the findings in regard to the relationship of the three groups toward their perceived incentives for and the barriers against contributing to UJA. Seven sets of factors were examined to see whether they could act as such incentives or barriers. They included the following: (1) being Jewish, (2) Israel, (3) anti-Semitism, (4) UJA image, (5) giving readiness, (6) solicitation context, and (7) financial situation. These seven themes were derived from the interviews based on questions suggested by UJA professionals and consultants as potentially the most revealing.

Note that any one factor could serve as a stimulus toward increasing the incentive to giving or raising the barrier to it. For example, respondents in the *Donors* group perceived the "UJA image/structure" as a potential barrier to giv-ing, even though they gave. Likewise, members of the *Unaffiliated* group saw the "UJA image/structure" as a real barrier to their giving. No one in these groups reported "UJA image/structure" as an incentive to giving. Nevertheless among the *Affiliated*, varying notions of "UJA image or structure" were per-ceived both as an incentive or barrier to giving for that group. Of course at the time of the research, that positive perception was not as evident as the negative one. A cell that had no response in it is marked "n.a." (not applicable).

The Donors

Of the seven different sets of factors identified, it was found that three could operate to produce perceived barriers toward giving to UJA even for the *Donors*.

Table 6.1 Orientations Toward Giving: Giving Valence (Perceived Incentives and Barriers to Giving) by Level of Affiliation for Donors, Affiliated, and Unaffiliated

Level of Affiliation	Giving Valence	
	Perceived Incentives (+)	Perceived Barriers (-)
	A	B
Donors	(1) Being Jewish: Identifying with Jewish community, Jewish organizations, Judaism and moral obligations (Mitzvah) of Tzedakah	(1) Being Jewish: n.a.
	(2) Israel: Trips and missions build identification with Israel	(2) Israel: n.a.
	(3) Anti-Semitism: Personal knowledge of Holocaust and awareness of anti-Semitism	(3) Anti-Semitism: n.a.
	(4) UJA Image/Structure: n.a.	(4) UJA Image/Structure: Elitist, wealthy, old (no room for young leadership), catering to big givers, exploitation of federation professional, Women's Division, don't know
	(5) Giving Readiness: Parent gave or relative benefits from UJA services	(5) Giving Readiness: n.a.
	(6) Solicitation Context: Charismatic speaker, inspirational professional, solicitation training, informational presentation, peer-group approval	(6) Solicitation Context: Public pledging, dinners, face-to-face, back-of-bus, phone, hard-sell techniques
	(7) Financial Situation: Reduction in inflation	(7) Financial Situation: Other financial obligations (Synagogue)
	C	D
Affiliated	(1) Being Jewish: Identifying with Jewish community, Jewish organizations, Judaism and moral obligations (Mitzvah) of Tzedakah	(1) Being Jewish: n.a.
	(2) Israel: Trips and missions build identification with Israel	(2) Israel: n.a.
	(3) Anti-Semitism: Awareness	(3) Anti-Semitism: n.a.
	(4) UJA Image/Structure: Need to know, cut out administrative middle-man	(4) UJA Image/Structure: Establishment, wealthy, old, distant, invisible, not relevant, Women's Division, don't know, don't rock the boat
	(5) Giving Readiness: n.a.	(5) Giving Readiness: n.a.
	(6) Solicitation Context: Emotional appeal, personal friend	(6) Solicitation Context: Public pledging, dinners, face-to-face, phone
	(7) Financial Situation: n.a.	(7) Financial Situation: No money, other financial obligations (JCC, Synagogue)

Table 6.1-Continued

	E	F
Unaffiliated	(1) Being Jewish: Moral obligation, sense of responsibility	(1) Being Jewish: Not interested in religious organizations, lack of Jewish identity, estrangement from religious life/Jewish culture
	(2) Israel: Emergency situation or crisis, identification or concern with Israel	(2) Israel: Policies of Israeli government
	(3) Anti-Semitism: Awareness	(3) Anti-Semitism: n.a.
	(4) UJA Image/Structure: n.a.	(4) UJA Image/Structure: Lack of knowledge of the UJA, not knowing what one's contribution actually does, wealthy sponsorship
	(5) Giving Readiness: n.a.	(5) Giving Readiness: n.a.
	(6) Solicitation Context: Emotional appeal, sense of duty, personal contact	(6) Solicitation Context: Phone calls, dinners, meetings, face-to-face, hard-sell
	(7) Financial Situation: n.a.	(7) Financial Situation: n.a.

For example, some of the images of UJA held by the *Donors* included: elitist, wealthy, old (no room for young leadership), catering to big givers, exploitation of federation professionals, having a Women's Division, or not familiar with UJA. Of course, many of these negative descriptions could also have been given by the *Unaffiliated* or the *Affiliated*. As one donor from Texas suggested:

> The problem I sometimes have is not understanding how the process is supposed to work in terms of decision. . . . I made one pledge. Then someone asked what about the Women's Division. My wife checked, and the pledge that I had made didn't count for that. . . .

Another donor from New York perceived UJA as distant and put it this way: "It's also a sense of something large and not connected to us." Occasionally a negative description emerges that could have come only from an insider, such as this observation about the treatment of the professional workers from a woman in New England:

> I think it's the nature of the beast. I think to work at a Jewish communal service organization like that and get paid *bubkas* ["peanuts"] and work with people who are dealing with millions and trillions of dollars—the whole volunteer versus professional psychology is absolutely wicked to deal with. I think a lot of the volunteers expect—because the communal service workers are getting paid—that they are, therefore, servants of some kind. There is very much that attitude which bothers me terribly. I think they take a terrible abuse. I can understand why someone who is very dynamic, wonderful, exciting, and inspirational would not want to stay in that kind of job and shouldn't. I get caught up in all that—sorry.

Another area that turned up as a barrier to the *Donors* was the solicitation context. Even in this group, there were objections to one form of solicitation or another, such as public pledging, dinners, face-to-face or back-of-bus techniques, phone calls, or hard sells. As one donor ventured, "I would dislike it if someone asked me to stand up at a meeting unless I agreed to it. Generally, I don't like a meeting where they are announcing gifts in groups."

Another donor objected to door-to-door solicitation: "I don't like a guy coming to me and tell[ing] me you owe me more than last year and arguing with me as they have done." And another observed: "It's okay if you want to get the fifty wealthiest guys in the community and let them throw dollars at each other; but if you are taking someone who is just starting out and he's at a dinner where everyone is pledging $1,000 and he had about $25 or $50 in mind, [then] I'm not going to go to any more dinners."

A final area of barriers for the *Donors* dealt with their financial situation. Usually, this took the form of conflicts between commitments to other Jewish institutions, such as the synagogue, and the UJA Campaign. As one man commented: "We cut back on UJA to make up for the synagogue (Building Fund) last year. We were kicked out of the computer for too much charitable deductions, and we have to go down there [IRS office] with all our receipts and canceled checks!" Lastly, here is the observation of a committed contributor lamenting her situation:

> We are becoming somewhat disenchanted with the fact that we sometimes feel that we are the only ones who are giving to the tune that we are giving, and when you find that nobody else is carrying the burden as heavily as you are, you stop and think what is wrong with me. Why am I so charitable and nobody else is? We cut back because we needed the money for something else [synagogue].

Nevertheless, these *Donors* gave, in some cases, with extreme generosity, to their local campaign. What prompted them to give? They gave largely, as noted before, for Jewish reasons. As one New Yorker stated, "I support Jewish institutions because I feel they are my protectors." Another was quoted as saying, "we are proud of the continuity of the past of the Jews who have preceded us, and we have to live up to their heritage, and we have to leave something to our children." Finally, one woman from New England saw her contributions as an element in affirming her Judaism in a broad sense:

> I'm trying to think of a realistic kind of education for the entire Jewish population of what it means to be a Jew that is not only to spend a day in the synagogue and pray. . . . There is a distinction in this country between social Judaism and religious Judaism. The two go hand in hand . . . [and] I mean a whole lot

more than tzedakah. I mean active participation. . . . There is a distinction between social means and religious means, and I think Jews have an obligation to
both.

In some instances, a particular Jewish experience was a motivating point for
giving, as in one Texan's participation on a Federation-sponsored mission to
Israel. This is how he reacted to it:

> The mission was the turning point. . . . Going to Israel has always been a
> dream. . . . I have seen the needs. I have to do it. For me, it's a Jewish responsi-
> bility. . . . The trip to Israel really made me understand what it all meant. I felt
> dignity while I was there. Something touched very deeply within me. Perhaps, I
> didn't know it was even there.

It should be pointed out that in most urban communities, the Federation at
the time of the study conducted one unified campaign for major Jewish charities
both nationally and locally. Historically, the greatest single beneficiary of the
fundraising effort was the United Jewish Appeal, which collected money on
behalf of the welfare causes in Israel. In New York, UJA and Federation were
separate entities for a long period of time. In recent years, many federations
have cut back on their allocations to Israel in favor of local groups, especially
when their revenues declined in the 1990s, due to the economic recession.

Sometimes there is a twin focus to the concerns of individuals—Israel and
anti-Semitism or the Holocaust. As one New Englander said, "There are two
things that keep us up at night: that is the security of Israel and having just read
or heard something about the Holocaust." A New Yorker was very concerned
about the situation of Soviet Jewry before the collapse of the Soviet Union:

> If you knew more Jews would get out . . . because of your contributions . . . you
> certainly would give more money. Indeed in some instances, the individuals re-
> ported feeling that some particular incident related to Israel or anti-Semitism
> was an especially powerful or peak experience: I was standing outside of the
> delivery room with G. [Holocaust survivor] . . . and they brought the baby [G's
> grandchild] . . . into the nursery. And G. and her friend started talking in Yid-
> dish about how they never in all those days in the camps ever thought they
> would live long enough to see their grandchildren and to stand there and share
> the experience of a grandchild being born, I mean . . . [choked with emotion] IT
> CAN'T HAPPEN AGAIN, EVER!

Finally, for some individuals, an additional motivating factor was their readiness to give, which resulted from their being socialized into a family oriented
toward contributing to the UJA Campaign. As one New Yorker observed, "If
there had to be any distinction that I had to make between givers and nongivers,
it would be to see what the parents did." Perhaps it was best summarized in this
way by one Floridian:

I came from a very modest family. It made me feel good to be giving to the Jewish Federation. It was something I was taught to be charitable. My mother and grandmother never turned anyone away. They came from an Orthodox family. To be able to be charitable made me feel good.

Does this evidence support the norm of reciprocity? In discussing motivational factors, respondents did not generally view their contributions as a quid pro quo for their receiving previous help. There is some indirect evidence for the norm of social responsibility in that it might be argued that the more Israel is seen as dependent on American Jews, the more people felt a need to contribute to the UJA, which supported, as a prime beneficiary, charitable needs in Israel. Perhaps a more comprehensive explanation exists in what might be dubbed the *"norm of social cohesion." By this is meant the following: The more people feel integrated into and identify with a particular community or subcommunity, the more likely they are to aid members or causes of their community or subcommunity perceived as in need of charitable contributions.*

The Affiliated

For the *Affiliated*, the same three general sets of factors operated as perceived barriers to giving, similar to the *Donors*. The difference was that the latter did not permit their perceptions to block their actions. This section will examine the situation of the *Affiliated* to see why they did not respond similarly.

One level of barriers reflected the problem of image and structure of UJA. The variety of negative images and perceptions was great. As one New Yorker said, "I get a sense from people that work there, and from my own perception (which may or may not be correct), that there is inefficiency in the staff and too much money goes in ways that aren't productive."

Another objected: "There is nothing really visible (of UJA) except for the phone calls. You never hear what happens if they made $100,000 last year. They have to show the Jewish community (what it does). . . . People have to see something tangible."

One Floridian was very blunt. He said, "The leadership is basically a bunch of old crotchety men who have retired and have nothing else to do but sit around and meet and hassle around the same issues." Another was disturbed by the concept of the Women's Division. She said: "They are not in touch with what the young Jewish woman sees and perceives . . . and they don't care." In another instance, a Texan saw the local Federation as not being sufficiently active:

I'm an old activist of a person. In college, I was very active mobilizing efforts for the Soviet Jews. I had the feeling many times that the UJA decision-making processes are stodgy. They don't want to rock boats. Many times, in order to accomplish things that need to be accomplished, they should go out on a limb a little; and they are unwilling to do that.

A New Yorker was opposed to the earlier merger of the Israel Campaign of UJA with the Federation Campaign for local needs:

> I don't think the merger of the Federation and UJA was a particularly good idea. You had two very (in my mind) dissimilar organizations. Federation was an organization that supported Jewish activities in this general area, whether it was hospitals, community centers, old-age homes. UJA is a support for Israeli organizations. Now the idea was that the same people basically give to both organizations, and therefore, a merging of the two would make one gift. I don't think that Federation-type activity has been helped by that particular merger. I feel that the Federation has been dominated more by UJA people than by Federation people, and it probably has lessened my sympathy with the organization as a whole.

One wonders what this individual would think of the national merger at the end of the 1990s of organizations that included the UJA! Another New Yorker volunteered this piece of advice: "UJA could get to me if I knew it wasn't a computerized business that makes me a number. I see UJA as a big, massive business." Finally, another man thought of the local Federation as less interested in cultivating potential young leaders than in coddling older big givers. He was rather frank in his statement: "To get the Federation board to agree to subsidize a young leadership commission took months of political hassling around. To get the Federation to spend $40,000 to lease a boat and bring on a caterer to have a handful of people give initial gifts which total $400,000—that they don't think twice about."

A second level of barriers reflected the concerns with solicitation techniques. One respondent from Florida stated: "I think the oral appeal affected me very early as a young man, or perhaps a teenager, in the synagogue High Holiday Services—the bidding for Torah honors. It was rather revolting, and I suppose that has carried with me." A New Yorker was also upset about solicitation techniques: "I can't set aside my personal offense at UJA methodology. I find it extraordinarily offensive. I think that what one gives is between himself and their Maker and not a matter of public consumption. . . ."

Finally, a third level of perceived barriers reflected the competitive strains of giving on the respondents' financial situation. A Floridian was most interested in contributing to an agency that appeared to give him the most "bang for the buck."

> I would rather give (my) money to . . . a programming agency rather than fundraising . . . you give to Federation once a year, fundraising time . . . but the

JCC is a year-round program. It's not as politically motivated. If things have to be done, they get done. They don't squander hours and hours debating an issue and making a mountain out of a molehill.

Another woman was interested in relevance. As she saw it, "People don't see the direct personal relevance in their everyday lives. To join a Temple is more related to their own practical family living." Another person saw the synagogue as the basis of a local communal identity as a Jew and, therefore, the practical necessity of supporting it. He said: "The synagogue is our top priority because we feel it is very important to maintain a visible, viable focal point in the community for having some support for Jewish traditions in a secular society, particularly in the public schools."

A New Yorker was rather introspective about the problem of giving money: "In some respects, money is always a problem in giving, and I guess there is always that feeling of 'I should have given more,' but that's only a feeling of my own compulsiveness and my own personality so that it is an unsatisfying experience."

Another New Yorker felt frustrated in giving: "What prevents people from giving? A feeling that no amount is really enough." Another person saw himself as philanthropic–and by the level of his reported contributions he was, but he did not see how UJA represented a potential beneficiary of his largesse. This is how he put it: "I'm philanthropic by nature, generally, and sometimes I'm concerned whether I have the ability to give as much as I would like. . . . Once I've committed myself it's just such a wonderful feeling, and that's the way I feel with the contributions I've made to the (humanitarian) project; and I'll go on to say as far as the contributions we've made to our Temple, I feel equally rewarded that I have done that."

For the *Donors* who did give and were involved in the UJA campaign, it would be difficult—even painful—to listen to people like the *Affiliated*, who were generous and contributing individuals both subjectively and objectively, but were not willing or able to include UJA in their circle of giving. Perhaps this was so because the Jewish identity of the latter was more "local" and oriented toward the particular synagogue or Jewish organization and that of the former was more "cosmopolitan," i.e., having a greater obligation to *klal yisrael*, or the totality of the Jewish people. Other evidence showed that the differences in Jewish identification were greatest comparing the *Donors* to the *Unaffiliated* rather than to the *Affiliated*.

What then were the incentives to giving perceived by the *Affiliated*? In many ways, these individuals seemed responsive to the same Jewish concerns as the *Donors*. The *Affiliated* generally felt a fairly strong sense of Jewish identification and even perceived the role of charitable giving in that sense of being

Jewish. As one Texan said, "I am Jewish and believe in being responsible for my community." Israel also played a role in their readiness to give. A Florida man suggested, "If I didn't like what I saw happening to Israel, I would definitely give more money." So what would encourage them to give? One level of incentives for giving perceived by the *Affiliated* was the Jewish level. As one *Affiliated* individual said, "Contributing to Jewish-oriented causes is more rewarding than others because of cultural, religious perceived ties." Indeed, the *Affiliated* were concerned about Israel. Indeed, the above person went on to say: "Money that goes specifically to help Israeli society in any way would be helpful. Anything that raises money to defend Israel strikes me as the most important organization. Israel is not only essential to all Jewish life, but it is essential to the future of Jewish life." Another said: "If they [the American government] don't support Israel, we have to. So the more negative the government is, the more positive and supportive of Israel we are."

In some instances, UJA was not perceived as the most appropriate vehicle to help Israel: "I would be far more interested in being charitable to an organization that is essentially Israeli in its nature and not created, conceptualized, whatever, from outside Israel." Another type of incentive was the need for more information about UJA. As one woman suggested, "If we know about the specifics [of UJA] in more detail [we would give]. . . . [We do] give [to our synagogue] because of our Jewish heritage." Another person seemed to suggest that the right kind of information could become an incentive for giving. He said, "Maybe there is an image problem. If it were better known what activities were available in our bedroom communities . . . we would support to a greater extent these activities . . . more activities that would involve the family."

In the area of the solicitation context, individuals offered suggestions as to what approaches might serve as incentives to giving for them and persons like themselves. One Floridian did not like the high-pressure approach: "Giving contributions . . . is basically a private matter. . . . [There should be] no requirement to give them despite a very professional and very slick approach. If you want to go home and think about it, you should have every right to do so."

Another felt that the appeal in the middle of a crisis was the best incentive to giving. When asked under what circumstances would people be most likely to give, he replied: "Wartime appeal when there is a crisis . . . because it's an emotional appeal. To say you have to support Israel when most people haven't been there. . . . It's hard for them to give [when] they have never come in contact with the Israeli culture, the historical background, never stood at the Wall."

Recent evidence suggested by Federation directors in the next chapter corroborated this testimony, as many professionals interviewed suggested that about one-quarter of gifts to the 2002 Israel Emergency Campaign came from new donors. A New Yorker suggested that an approach by the right person might work: "If someone you know asks you to give to something that is important to him, you do. It has to do with respecting his sense of value by requesting for a specific project."

One is tempted to conclude that even though the Affiliated had a good sense of Jewish identification, they were more selfish or less emotionally sensitive to the needs of their fellow Jews. This would seem unwarranted. Rather, it appeared that the overriding reason such people were not contributing to the Federation/UJA Campaign was because they did not see what their giving did for them locally. Their dollars may have done something for someone else in a distant location; but, they asked, what did it do for their immediate local needs as Jews? Thus, the Affiliated as noted above represented the "locals," whereas the Donors may be referred to as the "cosmopolitans." This was so because the latter had a broader view of their obligations to the larger community and, hence, were more cosmopolitan; the Affiliated took a narrower view and saw their obligations as more limited to their immediate local community.

The Unaffiliated

The Unaffiliated differed significantly from the other two groups in their Jewish characteristics. They had the least Jewish education; they were most likely to have no denominational preference (or something other than Orthodox, Conservative, or Reform) and they had the lowest level of synagogue attendance as noted by Lazerwitz, Winter, Dashefsky, and Tabory (1998) in their book on Jewish denominational choices. Hence, it was not surprising that a major barrier to their giving to UJA was their lack of Jewish identity. As a New Yorker said simply, "I feel no real identity." Another stated, "I don't feel a personal involvement as I would with some of the other things that people ask me to contribute to." A New Englander put it this way: "It is essentially a story of ineffective Jewish upbringing; partly the result of parents who were, of course, Jewish but not deeply committed, and were not able to give me any sense of inward identification with Judaism at home."

Finally, another New Yorker indicated his estrangement from Jewish life: "UJA is not part of my circle. . . . If I were involved with Jewish religious life, I think I would contribute. . . . I am completely estranged from that." A related barrier was the respondents' perceptions of Israel. A New Englander said: ". . . the UJA/Federation money, to my understanding, goes to Israel and as firm a supporter as I am to the people of Israel, I think some of the money goes to finance some of the 'crazy' things the government of Israel is doing."

Another put it this way: "I suspect that Israeli politics have become very central in determining how much people give or don't give. That could simply be a projection of what is on my own mind: the very recent aggressiveness."

(This sentiment was expressed in the 1980s at the time of the war in Lebanon, but could easily apply in the twenty-first century to some of the responses of the Israeli government in the conflict with the Palestinians.) At another level of concern was the familiar problem expressed by *Donors* and *Affiliated* as well—the image or structure of UJA. One New Yorker voiced a recurrent theme: "I don't understand the structure of Jewish charities. I don't know what UJA does." Another wondered: "I don't know how much money goes to run the organization, and how much gets paid to fundraisers, and how much actually filters down to charity after bureaucracy gets through with it." Finally, another New Yorker seemed more hostile: "Does my contributing to UJA foster the very forces in Jewish life that I am against? That's my real concern. Am I giving to the enemy so to speak."

A New England resident suggested: "One reason people don't give is that they don't know anything about it. It is not high on their priority list." Another said: "People of my age have left—and I feel in distressing numbers—due to a communication problem, or what I suspect that part of it is a matter of image . . . and I'm not sure the organization communicates very well with the assimilated Jews such as myself who nonetheless consider themselves Jews."

A third level of barriers reflected concerns with solicitation techniques. One New Yorker offered the following statement: "I don't want someone pushing the button on my door or [calling on] the telephone. I tend to be turned off by that. It's a sales pitch, like anything else, like selling soap." Another complained: "It's the pressure part that I don't like, more than anything else. You are being asked to make a decision too quickly. Someone is using their personal relationship with me for reasons other than their relationship with me."

Another kind of barrier related to solicitation was voiced by a New England woman: "(They) consistently refer to women by their husband's name. It made me totally angry, despite the fact that she may have accomplished a great deal. I would hope that they would have a consciousness of the contemporary woman." A New England man objected to the pressure of solicitation: "I personally resent anyone telling me I have to give, and I think part of the good feeling of giving is wanting to give, and I would not get that if someone said I had to unless it was a dire emergency."

Finally for some individuals, there was the financial barrier. As one Florida man said: "People just don't have the money; it's getting increasingly more difficult to make ends meet. When you're struggling to keep your head above water, it makes it a little harder to think outside of your immediate circle."

Despite the fact that the *Unaffiliated* group had a lower level of Jewish identification, their sense of being Jewish generally remained alive, as indicated earlier. A New Yorker said, "No matter what is going on in our life, good, bad, whatever, we have always felt a definite responsibility." Another was very concerned about the plight of Jewry abroad: "I would love to know how I could contribute to their welfare in any way. . . . I'm most conscious of those Jews in danger." In another instance, anti-Semitism was seen as a motivating factor. "If I begin to perceive anti-Semitism as a real threat, I would once again begin to give to Jewish causes a lot more liberally than I am now."

In addition, some of these *Unaffiliated* individuals were also very concerned about Israel—especially if they perceived an emergency: "If, God forbid, there was going to be a war tomorrow and Israel needed planes or something, then obviously we would do everything we could to help." Another affirmed: "I would feel a commitment to help preserve the State of Israel." Indeed, some individuals may contribute but only during wartime: "I suppose the UJA appeal at that time perhaps gave me a sense of satisfaction that I did something. It brought home a lot of memories. It brought to mind a lot of things that I feel I contribute in terms of Israel." The implication of these findings is the need to first cultivate that sense of Jewishness, however vaguely defined.

Some individuals saw the need for a certain type of solicitation context. One Floridian said: "It's more non-threatening for you to talk to a personal contact, someone you might know, than if someone knocks at the door." A New England resident suggested a similar theme of solicitation by the "image maker" or "significant other," the person influential in shaping the thinking of the solicited person:

> If I got a letter addressed to me from [the prime minister of Israel] asking me for money, I would probably find it hard to turn down. If [it were] someone of personal importance . . . you would be hard pressed to turn it down. Not from the mass mailing, no, like from *Reader's Digest*; but if something was impressed upon me as being of great need, I would give it considerable consideration.

Another type of incentive mentioned by one of the *Unaffiliated* was the possibility of offering a non-monetary contribution. Perhaps this was more consistent with the financial situation of the individual as was reported. "I am more inclined to spend time, rather than money, for causes I believe in."

Summary

In Chapter Four, the similarities between the characteristics of the respondents in the smaller, more qualitative phase of the research (including *Donors*, *Affiliated* and *Unaffiliated*) and the larger, quantitative National Jewish Population Surveys (described in Chapter Three) were documented. In Chapter Five, more details were revealed about the orientations of the three groups, which indicated how *Donors'* prior Jewish socialization experiences and contemporaneous communal involvement led them to contribute and the *Unaffiliated* to abstain from such donations, while the *Affiliated* lacked a sympathetic understanding of what UJA or Jewish Federation did. In this chapter, more details were revealed about the incentives and barriers to charitable giving for the three groups.

In sum, the *Unaffiliated* shared with the *Donors* and *Affiliated* similar concerns about the barriers they perceived to their contributing to UJA with respect to its image or structure and solicitation techniques. Where the *Unaffiliated* differed significantly from the *Donors* and *Affiliated* was in the barrier that their lower level of Jewish identification posed. In respect to incentives for giving, they perceived that certain Jewish concerns might arouse their consciousness toward charitable giving, such as Israel or anti-Semitism. Without further cultivation of their sense of Jewishness, these charitable gifts might only be forthcoming from some in an emergency situation. Thus, the evidence suggested that the "norm of social cohesion" applied more strongly to those individuals (*Donors* and, to a lesser extent, *Affiliated*) who had a stronger personal identity as a community member than those who had a weaker personal identity (*Unaffiliated*); and this norm may operate to lead individuals to make contributions.

Note:

1. Parts of this chapter were adapted with permission of the publisher from Arnold Dashefsky. "American Pluralism and the Jewish Community." Pp. 203–25 in Seymour Martin Lipset (ed.), *American Pluralism and the Jewish Community*. New Brunswick, NJ: Transaction. Copyright © (1990) by Transaction Publishers.

Chapter Seven

Twenty-first Century Realities:
The Views of the Fundraising Directors[1]

Given that the three groups, *Donors*, *Affiliated*, and *Unaffiliated*, described in the previous chapter, were interviewed in the 1980s, it would be desirable to determine whether their responses are still relevant in the twenty-first century. Rather than search out this same group of individuals or another group of similar individuals, a different but complementary track was traced. A group of twenty-five professional fundraising directors in the Jewish community, drawn from the national office of the United Jewish Communities (or UJC, successor organization to the United Jewish Appeal) as well as executive directors of over twenty local Jewish community federations,[2] whose combined Jewish population represented more than three-quarters of American Jewry, was interviewed.

These 25 interviews were gathered during the period 2000–03. Some interviews were conducted prior to the events of September 11, 2001, and the Passover attack in Israel in the spring of 2002 (n=12) and some following these events (n=13), which afforded an opportunity to assess their potential impact on fundraising in the Jewish community. Each respondent was asked a series of eight to twelve key questions, which were subsequently coded. Then the coded responses were grouped together to ascertain the relative frequency of responses to the battery of questions asked.

A main focus of the interviews was to assess the incentives and barriers to charitable giving in the Jewish community in twenty-first-century American society as seen through the eyes of the professional fundraisers drawn from both the national and local levels. Included in this analysis was an assessment of the extent to which the responses of the *Donors*, *Affiliated*, and *Unaffiliated*, cited in the previous chapter, were still relevant in the contemporary period.

Positive Directions in Fundraising

Each respondent was informed that the purpose of the interview was to understand to what extent the patterns that had been previously discerned by inter-

101

viewing *Donors*, *Affiliated*, and *Unaffiliated* had changed both at the macro-level of the community and the micro-level of the individual and to assess any new directions based on their experience in the world of Jewish federations. Toward that purpose, the interview began with a probe of the positive directions for American Jewish fundraising in the first decade of the twenty-first century. The most frequent responses focused on the *financial ability and personal desire to give*, with 44 percent of respondents offering this factor as a positive direction. As one respondent stated, "There are almost limitless resources. Wealth creation in the last decade [1990s] is 'under' understood." The respondent continued, "Why do people rob banks? Answer: That is where the money is. [Therefore,] wealth creates a dream scene for Jewish fundraisers." The respondent then went on to point out that federation endowment funds now have assets of $8 billion and Jewish sponsored family foundations, numbering perhaps seven thousand, have another $12 billion, which include executives from major high tech firms like Dell, Microsoft, and Sysco. The growth in wealth, the executive suggested, will lead to a growth in foundations.

Another respondent pointed out that some wealthy donors have an interest in using their funds to support Jewish identity, but another fundraiser suggested that the annual campaign and appeal to individuals can only bring results to a certain level and there is a need to reach the "mega-donors" and the wealthy family foundations. Other respondents emphasized that Jews as a whole are wealthier now than in the past and that there continues to be more money. "The most positive thing is that the campaign in gross dollars is growing marginally (and) the endowment portion continues to pick up speed; that is very positive," concluded another respondent.

Another major positive direction mentioned by 40 percent of the executives is the *entrepreneurial direction* of Jewish giving. One executive noted that a generational change was at work. Whereas for the older half of the population, including older boomers, the notion of tzedakah resonated very well, this concept does not work well with the younger segments of the population. For them, the concept of "opportunity" is a catchword, replacing the word "responsibility," used to attract the older generation. The "younger generation wants to get something in return. They are willing to listen and learn when we give them something in return." Along these lines, another respondent suggested that "philanthropy is moving to a business model." While "the consumer mentality is often viewed as negative . . . people will invest in it . . . if we show the relevance of the system to everyday life." As another executive suggested, "Federation needs to create an apparatus for entrepreneurs, family foundations, grant money, corporate money, and one-time giving. The community needs to develop standards for each." Finally as one fundraiser concluded, "From an economic perspective, the generation[al] transfer of wealth is a positive indication of growth potential."

Additional factors identified by one-third to one-sixth of the executives as positive directions for American Jewish fundraising were quite varied. More frequently noted by one-third of the respondents was the observation that *involvement by young people in the campaign was emerging*. As one director stated, "Generation X [twenty-two to thirty-five year olds] is becoming involved in the Jewish community. This category's proportional increase is the greatest. [Therefore, I'm] not worried about the fate of the community in ten years. . . . Young people and entrepreneurs want to make investments in Israel." Another added:

> It is still possible to turn our people to Federated giving and giving in general. It may not be at the gut level; once they see what they can give to, then their giving will be stronger. We have to educate them to what the dollars do. "Touch—not trust" is what we tell our young professional staff people. For the previous generation, trust was enough. Today, trust is not enough, people have to see it. A mission to Israel is more important today than twenty-five years ago because then people knew the time when there was no Israel or overseas agenda; our work is much different [today] than ten years ago. Then, the donors had very little to say over what happened to their money. We have changed how we've allocated money over the years. We talk about [our] projects in Israel. If it weren't for [us], Ethiopian kids wouldn't be ready for kindergarten.

Another executive also spoke to this point:

> We've had success in the younger generation, but [we] need more money. It is possible to reach them: Young leaders are starting to give $5,000–10,000 through dinner parties and educational meetings. We can create an elite tone that engages young leaders. A lot don't have a family tradition of Jewish philanthropy. A lot of them are self-made who came from a comfortable upper-middle class Jewish lifestyle, but their parents weren't into philanthropy. This is a newer commitment [of] the younger generation. When they go overseas, it is a life-changing experience.

Another fundraiser agreed that "contrary to [the popular] view, younger people are . . . involved," but not all. "Some in their thirties and forties are turned on and involved and some are not." Further testimony to this effect was offered by the following observation: "In most communities, there's an increasing number of young people who stand up and identify Jewishly. In the last eight to ten years, young people are willing to support Jewish causes." In sum, to paraphrase what one executive observed: "the younger generation is more involved in 'recreational spirituality,' which is replacing 'obligatory Jewish giving' by 'value-driven Jewish giving.'"

Among the factors that were mentioned by one-quarter of respondents were two items. The first focused on the *creation of a sense of community and the search for meaning and spirituality*. As one respondent stated, "In this generation, which gets put down as not community-minded and loyal, we found that when we invest in good leadership, they are as good as the previous leaders. We invested more in the professional and volunteer leadership [because] everything is dependent on leadership." Another put it this way: "A core group of people care about the Jewish community for its continuity and values and for its contribution to society at large. Therefore, those people will invest in the Jewish community. The older generation continues to feel that way."

The second factor referred to by one-quarter of respondents was the nature of multi-faceted giving, i.e., *there is a need to have multiple approaches to the diversity of givers*. For example, one respondent reviewed a variety of issues concerning this positive feature of twenty-first-century fundraising and stated that some donors are:

> more interested in understanding than philanthropy. More people have made more money and now there is more money but a greater diversity in Jewish giving. [There is a] more sophisticated donor group [and we] need to work to keep them. Donors are underrated in influencing a cause and consumers have more knowledge. Most grow up in a world where giving was more automatic. [For example,] if an Israeli wore his colonel uniform, people would give automatically. We give more information on the causes we fund but don't believe in designated giving. For major donors, we want one charitable advisor (layperson or professional) for each major donor. We give them a plan for annual giving or estate planning. Our approach is like the change from a salesperson to a financial planner.

Another executive saw it this way, "The challenge for fundraising is for us to understand the donors and what their interests are. [However,] there are regional differences and some of the West Coast people are interested in services moving west."

The multi-faceted nature of twenty-first-century Jewish giving means, as one fundraiser saw it, that "many people are giving philanthropy rather than tzedakah." In sum, there is a "perspective of personal development [and we] need to look critically at how we have changed and see how to approach the individual. [We] need to adapt and adjust and be creative and aggressive in looking to raise money" is what another fundraiser concluded.

A variety of other issues was mentioned by about one-fifth or less of the sample as positive directions for American Jewish fundraising in the twenty-first century. They included the following:

1. *designated giving;*
2. *creation of mega-foundations; and the*
3. *continued responsiveness of American Jews to an emergency situation which threatens a particular community.*

As one executive stated: "The Jewish community still responds well to emergencies. You can still touch their souls if the community is in danger. People who do not often give may give to the emergency campaign, for example, Israel and Argentina." But another continued that the creation of large Jewish foundations poses a potential problem:

> An increasing number of Jewish Family Foundations and Federations, which contribute to various Jewish causes, have stimulated us to get connected with them to tell them about our interests. The caution is that our institutions depend on unrestricted funds. We might end up with too many restricted funds.

Surprisingly two perennial magnets for attracting Jewish dollars, Israel and, more recently, Jewish education, were only mentioned by a very few as positive directions in the twenty-first century. Israel was mentioned in connection with the 2002 Israel Emergency Campaign in the wake of the Passover attack of that year but not as the spark that ignited fundraising beginning in 1967 after the Six-Day War. Perhaps Jewish education—particularly Jewish day schools—were seen in the twenty-first century as a competitive threat, rather than a positive direction for the Federations in American Jewish philanthropy in the twenty-first century.

Negative Directions in Fundraising

The responses to this issue of negative directions in fundraising were more clearly tiered than was the case in the previous question. At the highest level of consensus, about one-half of the executives' responses focused on the Jewish federation's profile with regard to the *1) quality of professionals, 2) the mission, goals, and vision, and 3) the methods employed in the conduct of their work.*

One fundraising director, in citing the third point noted above about methods employed, argued that it is "more expensive to raise money: Salaries are higher and donors are concerned about overhead. [It is] hard to find good staff and donors are concerned about administrative expenses." Another observed:

> [We] need to chew gum and talk at the same time. We need to build torah and tzedakah, but we also need to increase penetration. In five congregations, giving increased 25 percent while the overall [communal] increase was 12 percent. People who knew us loved us more. UJC says to do mass marketing as if [we're] selling *Newsweek* magazine [which means] call them once. [But] I want to create a community network. [Our federation] is more like the Avon Lady or Tupperware. We need networks of community [and] we need to use our networks [while] we need to respect the dignity of individuals.

A different approach was taken by an executive who saw both the positive and negative in the Federation movement: "If communities had done all the planning, all day schools would be Orthodox. [There needs to be a] balancing of how much [goes to] Israel and how much domestic, but Federations need to be heavy-handed in their decisions and not very consultative." Likewise, another saw it this way: "Federation is perceived as a bureaucracy and this inhibits giving. People don't see the value added of community planning." Another director saw the negative ramifications of highly publicized scandals in fundraising: "Accountability of fundraising and scandals of charitable organizations make people more discerning. People want to give more directly."

The issue of staff needs at Federations was also noted by an executive who stated, "We're not doing a good job in preparing professionals. We are not getting the brightest and the best. Our training is not that good. We have twenty-five to thirty years of joint programs and it is not helping." This observation was supported by another who declared: "[There is a] real lack of emphasis on quality professionals and development of professionals in the field. People coming in are highly qualified but lack experience in the field." Following up on the latter point, another suggested that "the professional field is increasingly women. If some numbers of men are not involved, then it will be harder for men to give."

A similar proportion of about one-half of executives was concerned about the possible negative directions of the *competitiveness among charities—both with other Jewish as well as non-Jewish charities*. The competitive threat from general community organizations was voiced by another fundraiser:

> The big gorilla is that Jewish leaders are welcome and aggressively sought by general community, non-profits. That's a huge challenge for us. We're not as good as many other organizations in welcoming them and thanking them and recognizing their contributions. We have a high bar to be a significant leader.

Another executive noted that there was much "competition within the Jewish community for giving money to many Jewish causes. People are confused as to when to give; loyalties are not as strong. Jews are accepted everywhere and [the executive added, referring to the previous issue] we are facing competition from non-Jewish causes." Another fundraiser observed that "there is greater potential for competition among Jewish organizations. Relatively few Jewish organizations are unworthy of support; about 150 separate Jewish fundraising campaigns [exist] each year and about half are Israeli." As was presented in Chapter Three, more donations from American Jews go to general causes than Jewish causes, a fact noted by one of the interviewees. A colleague noted that many gifts go to general causes, e.g., the arts, higher education and health care. Another executive put it bluntly: "Mega-donors are making gifts everywhere but not to the Jewish community. No one gave an $11 million gift to the Jewish community, but one did to a prestigious private university."

The problem, noted one director, is that there is "huge competition. Many Jewish organizations are using Federation techniques to reach the people and raise money. Donors like the clarity of the single cause. The multi-faceted value of Federation is not an alternative. There is a great skepticism." Furthermore, the

Jewish community appears to be moving away from communitarianism, as another executive observed.

At a lower level of concern shared by about one-quarter to one-third of executives was a variety of *issues reflecting changes in American Jewry, including the perceived self-centeredness or "me-focus" of the younger generation and the degree of assimilation of the community.* Other changes noted were the *lack of loyalty to the community, the decline of anti-Semitism, and the loss of distinctiveness, "rampant individualism," contentiousness over the policies of the Israeli government, the decline of Jewish neighborhoods, and increased fragmentation.* As one executive observed: "People are not joiners. We all need to watch TV together as a family, but today everyone individually has a television."

These changes in American society and Jewry seem to be most keenly felt in regard to the younger generation: "[There is] not much passion in fundraising, people gave off the back of Israel. Young people do not worry that there will not be an Israel and did not live through the Holocaust," said one executive. Another observed that the "intergenerational commitment is not being transmitted. The new generation lacks a strong commitment to the Jewish people and Jewish life." Furthermore, "the changing dynamics of American culture [means that] 'umbrella giving' does not resonate well among younger givers. [There is also a] big issue of trust although we have not done anything to earn mistrust."

The culture of America and, consequently, American Jews appears to be dominated by "materialism and individualism." Therefore, potential donors are perceived to be "in pursuit of wealth and status." As one executive observed, "Philanthropy is a big word. It could reflect a deep abiding care for others, but it could also be narcissistic. We're in pursuit of wealth and status and live in an age of materialism and individualism."

Another negative noted was the *process of assimilation,* which was seen as evident by one respondent in the "increasing disconnect between North American Jewry and World Jewry" (except in the case of the 2002 Israel Emergency Campaign) and the "increasing disconnect between individual Jews and the Jewish community." Another executive saw the negative in "assimilation, outmarriage and disaffiliation with Jewish life. We see a massive fleeing outward; but, at the same time, we see a growth in the core of Jewish institutions." Despite the rise in intermarriage, another executive also saw that there were opportunities: "Interfaith couples have a tenuous connection to the organized Jewish community and it will take more resources to get them involved."

Another area of negative directions observed by about one-quarter of respondents was the concern expressed about "*designated giving.*" This approach allows the donors to exercise control over the dollars by allowing them to earmark funds for a specific donor organization within the Federation umbrella. This approach is akin to the general community appeals which permit donors to specify that a portion of their gifts may go to the Red Cross, Urban League, or perhaps the local Jewish Community Center. The concern of some directors is that "donor designation will drive communal allocations" as one put it. Ultimately, the problem is one of how much control should the organized local community, operating through the allocations committees, surrender to individual donor choices. The whims of the latter may not coincide with the planning process of the former. One executive expressed the reservations of some directors most succinctly: "If restricted funds get too great, then giving can go in a negative way. If designated giving gets out of control, there won't be funds for smaller institutions." Another executive expressed concerns in this way:

> [Re] designated giving, our Federation has a policy which discourages our board from designated giving to the United Way. Our task is to take care of the whole community. There is no evidence that designated giving raises more money. The United Way did it because corporate leadership forced them into it. A sub-theme to designated giving [is that] we have gone heavily into donor-advised funds. [One-third came] from annual campaign out of [the total] granted and the [other two-thirds] was from grants from supporting foundations and donor advised funds. . . . It's good news. We're bearing the administrative cost for people to give money to all funds [including non-Jewish ones].

Another area of concern which was viewed as a negative was voiced by about a quarter of respondents and dealt with the *changing demographics of American Jewry*. One director offered this observation:

> Most of our gifts come from those sixty and older. Young people give more modestly. They have a sophisticated professional knowledge but a simplistic knowledge of Jewish life. They laugh at anti-Semitism, don't feel a connection to the State of Israel, and are not excited about synagogues.

Recognizing these changes, another executive volunteered that "we have not changed, but the population has changed." A different cautionary theme was struck by another executive who observed: "[There is a] shift in the view that grandparents believed their children would be better off; but the grandchildren might not be better off than the parents. The youngest generation may not have the sense of security to be able to give." The aging process of the community, therefore, was producing

> big generation gaps. [We are] losing the core of major gifts due to age and attrition. The older generation, for whom giving was a core of their life, can't at this stage of the life cycle increase giving. Younger people have not emerged to replace them. [It is] a lot easier to reach a handful of beginner givers. The new gifts may never reach the level of the older givers.

There was a smattering of other responses offered in each case by less than one-fifth of the sample. They included the *decrease in the quality of gifts and the decline in the economy.* While many mentioned the increasing assimilation, only a small number specifically mentioned *a disconnect from Israel and World Jewry.* Some of these concerns were allayed by the response to the Israel Emergency Campaign of 2002.

Grounds for Optimism

Despite the perceived negative directions in American Jewish fundraising, many professionals were optimistic about American Jewry and American Jewish fundraising. At the top of the list was the *wealth available to a significant portion of the community* as expressed by 42 percent of respondents. The three NJPS studies of 1971, 1990, 2000–01 have consistently shown that American Jewish households have an estimated annual family income that is larger than the reported income for the United States population.

One federation executive described the situation based on a "significant optimism for Jewish philanthropy. [We] need to allow individuals to meet their own philanthropic desires. This will lead to growth in philanthropy." Another's source of optimism was based on the assumption that "large sums of money are available, and, if educated, people will give." Along these lines, another executive exclaimed: "It is still pretty spectacular (in reference to fundraising). We raise more than the United Way."

At the next level of salience were the executives' perceptions of a *strong Jewish identity among many community members*, a notion supported by one-third of respondents. What made this many executives assert such optimism despite the negative trends identified in the previous section? An "increased emphasis on Jewish literacy, Jewish camping, and Jewish education," said one. "Enormous signs of reawakening in Jewish identity," said another, emphasizing the growth of Hillel at a nearby university. Another executive observed the following: "All the conditions that I see show that Jews have a need for spiritual meaning in their lives. The past few years have been a golden age of Jewish publishing. It is a sign of a golden age of Jewish awareness and growth. There is a real search for meaning."

One executive's optimism was rooted in the "resurgence of interest in Jewish life. As identity increases, Jewish giving does also. In the old days, you could get a big gift from someone who didn't give a damn about Jewish life. They gave because their family gave." The sense of changes taking place in Jewish identity characterized another's optimism: "American Jewry is undergoing redirection and is more concerned about Jewish identity. [This is] especially [true] among people in [their] thirties and forties who have young children. [We see a] growth of day schools . . . youth groups, and camping programs. This will lead to a stronger Jewish identity."

Another prominent set of responses, voiced by more than one-fourth of interviewees, focused on the sense of optimism about Jewish life that they felt. Some responses were based on a faith assumption, rooted in the traditional expression, *netzah yisrael lo yishaker* ("the eternity of the Jewish people will not be negated"), as in this respondent's answer: "I'm an optimist by nature. We'll find the resources to meet our community's needs." This sentiment was echoed by another fundraiser:

> There is a lot of vitality and experimentation within a small committed core. Those Jews who are seriously committed are more engaged than in a prior generation. That fuels new emotion. The core is more interested in serious study and engaging their families in Jewish life.

A different respondent offered this observation:

> I'm optimistic because I believe that logic prevails. If we say that we are a diminishing population, then people will eventually understand it and work together. We need to educate young people why it is worth being Jewish. If they don't know it, they won't be it. Intelligent people act intelligently.

Finally, another offered this optimistic assessment coupled with a historical rationale:

> By nature I'm an optimist—otherwise I wouldn't work for the Jewish community. Without Jews, the world would be in great trouble. I don't know that I am optimistic long term about the Federation [because] *the only institution that has endured is the synagogue. To the extent that Federations create a coalition in synagogues, I am optimistic* [italics for emphasis].

One other area of optimism, to which one-quarter of respondents alluded, was the *strong connection to Israel*, which still appeared to endure despite the ongoing tensions surrounding the conflict with the Palestinians. About one-half of the interviews were completed in the wake of the "Passover massacre" in the spring of 2002. Despite the concerns many American Jews held about the government in Israel at that time, the great majority perceived the purpose of the Intifada, or Palestinian uprising, as an attempt to delegitimate the State of Israel. Therefore, a Federation executive stated that "Israel resonates strongly with people—that connection to the land and peoplehood. [Consequently,] we are running another Israel Emergency Campaign." The second campaign, an optional one conducted in 2003, was a follow-up to the one all Federations conducted in 2002.

Indeed, the Intifada may have strengthened the commitment of American Jews to Israel even though tourism from the United States had declined. Consider this observation by an executive:

Israel's precarious situation has caused both Israel and American Jews to gain a greater understanding of why we need each other to survive. In the late 1990s, we were forgetting how important Israel is to our survival. We have thousands who weren't donors, [but now] thousands of students on college campuses are motivated to support Israel.

Other optimistic responses which were offered by one-sixth or less of respondents included the following:

1. *sense of accomplishments of the Jewish community;*
2. *growth of interest in Jewish studies at colleges;*
3. *spirit of community; and the*
4. *emergence of younger givers.*

Pessimistic Responses

Despite the aroused optimism expressed by the fundraising executives as noted above, there were also pessimistic expressions about American Jewry and its philanthropic endeavors. At the apex of pessimism was the *increasing assimilation of American Jews*, which was identified by 36 percent of respondents. The tension created by the tendency toward assimilation was raised by one executive, who pondered the question: "How do we function as a unique ethos in a pluralistic society? We're lucky to live in a free place. Assimilation is inevitable, but we haven't figured that out."

Assimilation has been hastened by the breakdown in barriers that once excluded Jews from participation in the elite echelons of society, including charitable organizations, which led one executive to observe: "We are competing in a society that actively seeks out Jews." Another executive lamented that the agenda is enormous:

It's so complex. There are so many battles to be won—so much politics and rebuilding. It's easy to be depressed. I'm essentially an optimist, [but] there is an incredible weariness. Assimilation and intermarriage are recognized by American Jewry as a condition of American Jewish life.

A colleague echoed this sentiment and observed: "Intermarriage is not good for continuity. Two generations out from intermarriage and 99 percent of grandchildren do not identify as Jews. The power of a free and open society is greater than what the Jewish community can do." A different fundraiser took a more reserved, realistic position: "Intermarriage is a reality; a more embracing community could overcome it. Some intermarried couples are going into young leadership."

At the next level of pessimistic concern, noted by one-third of respondents, was the issue of *the quality of professionals entering or leaving the fields and the strength of the Federation movement*. As one fundraiser observed:

> Jewish communal federation executives are leaving to go somewhere else—to do something else. They go to the Foundation world. The creation of Foundations cuts two ways: The negative is less centrality of fundraising and the positive is long-term money for Jewish causes. [This development has] created a new clan of royalty—"Foundation Holders"—and it is a mixed bag.

A colleague echoed this sentiment:

> We are failing to attract the best and brightest [Jewish community professionals] into our field. . . . Day schools are desperate for professional workers and the numbers of graduates produced by the "Hornstein Programs" [dual-degree programs in social work and communal service like the Hornstein Program at Brandeis University] are minuscule.

At a more macro-level, an executive observed that the: "Federation movement needs to restructure and rethink. The local Federation needs to rethink what they are doing. The annual campaign is only one modality as fundraising is a means to an end–money to build community."

Another source of discouragement was the "infighting that goes on—the battle over turf between agencies and lack of good layperson-professional relations." Nevertheless, the words of one colleague would likely be embraced by many: "There's no point to be a pessimist but [rather to] be sober [and to] be an optimist and [yet to] be disappointed some of the time."

At a somewhat lower level of concern was the perceived need for a *partnership to build the community*, a notion embraced by one-quarter of the professionals. One way to build the community, as noted by one executive, was the "need to build a connection to synagogues; at our Super-Sunday, we will split any new gifts with the congregation. . . . We designated $100,000 for a synagogue initiative."

Another executive saw the challenge of the community in this way: "If Jewish community resources are not put into developing a vision for the future, then we are going to be in trouble. If we don't plan for the future, we'll suffer. If we don't develop a Jewish education system and invest in people to tie them to their Jewish heritage, then we will be out." A third added that "we have not been able to mobilize our resources on a continental level." Another consequence of the communal disconnect, observed another professional, had to do with World Jewry. "So much of the life and death issues are overseas [for example, the difficult economic circumstances experienced by Jews in Argentina at the time of the interview]. If people don't have the connection, they don't care about giving to causes abroad."

Additional pessimistic answers were expressed in the concern to *broaden the appeal of Federations* by one-quarter of interviewees. As one professional stated: "[We] may well have lost a generation because of lack of programs to bolster Jewish identity; therefore, we experience much assimilation and inter-marriage. These programs won't completely reverse the trends, [but] I believe that we have turned the corner."

The practical problem that emerges from a narrow base of the community was identified by another professional in that it is "harder to raise money be-cause you have to broaden your base." In the course of the interviews, various segments of the market for donations were identified as difficult to reach in some communities, including forty-five to sixty year olds, academics, and, per-haps, of greater concern, the "super-rich." One executive stated it baldly: "The billionaires don't see organized Jewish communities as a place to put an enorm-ous component of their giving. We don't seem to be able to get them to invest in us." Furthermore, among the older good givers, there was a "failure of genera-tional continuity in Jewish contributions—older to younger giver." The wealthy parents who gave generously were not as likely to have offspring who gave as generously when they reached a similar maturity.

A variety of other responses was noted by interviewees, but they came from less than one-fifth of the sample. They included problems with giving among *the younger generation who were viewed as too self-centered or materialistic*: "The new generation emerging is narcissistic, not as compassionate as the generation who preceded them," argued one fundraiser. *Competition from other charitable causes was noted here*: "Big donors are not supporting the community campaign in the way they should. They are supporting art museums or specific Jewish causes, like day schools. They're going after recognition in the non-Jewish world."

Other issues expressed less consistently by the fundraisers had to do with the *faddishness of fundraising causes* which shifted across time, the *decline of Israel and anti-Semitism as magnets for money*, the *trend toward individualism which "overwhelms the obligation to philanthropy,"* and the *"lack of Jewish education and understanding of Jewish heritage,"* which was exacerbated in the minds of a few by the *increase in intermarriage*. Finally, and most interesting, only one respondent mentioned the *decline in the economy* at the beginning of the twenty-first century as a source of pessimism.

The Effects of Terror on Fundraising

About one-half of the interviews were gathered in 2000 and 2001 prior to the terrorist attack on the United States on September 11, 2001, and the Passover attack in Israel in the spring of 2002 and one-half after these events. The inter-views conducted in the second half of 2002 and 2003 added questions about the impact of these events on fundraising.

In regard to the question on ways that fundraising changed in the wake of 9/11/2001, the Federation executives did not report a significant impact. Only a few offered any substantive observations. One professional observed that "In the beginning, it was a negative since people were concerned about their own physical danger and did not care about others." Another suggested that "in some very specific issue-oriented areas, fundraising was aided, for example, increasing institutional security and addressing issues on college campuses; [but some] diminished giving has also occurred as a kind of communal post-traumatic stress disorder."

One executive offered a more general observation about the impact of 9/11: "The power of 9/11—a clash of civilizations—has impacted on the arts. They're nice things, but people supported human needs." Finally, another executive observed a constructive outcome: "There's been a positive shift in terms of fundraising. We've raised more money. We created an immediate response level. We worked through our agencies for people having [suffered] traumas."

In general, it is fair to say that most respondents who replied to this question saw no change or connection resulting from the tragedy of 9/11. A minority saw a new or strengthened connection-based on the vulnerability and pain people felt and suffered—especially to Israel.

Responses to the question on the *effects of the Israel Emergency Campaign (IEC)* initiated in the wake of the terrorist attack in Israel on a group of Jews celebrating Passover (or Pesah) in a public venue *were more numerous* among those professionals who were queried. More than three-quarters of respondents reported that Israel re-emerged as a high priority for funding. Re-emerged is an appropriate term because for much of the last one-half to one-third of the twentieth century, especially after the Six-Day War in June 1967, Israel was the main magnet for attracting funds to the local Jewish federations and the former United Jewish Appeal campaigns. This magnetism began to weaken in the 1980s and 1990s as a result of a growing disenchantment with the policies of the Israeli government as well as an emergent recognition of the needs of the American Jewish community for "continuity," "renewal," and "renaissance."

Nearly two-thirds of respondents reported funding for Israel became a high priority that produced quick results. As one executive reported:

> We were one of the first to start an IEC. We wanted to raise $2 million and in six months we had our goal. [Then the] Pesah massacre [April 2002] happened and . . . we went from $1.8 million to $5 million in three weeks after the Pesah massacre. . . . The clear lesson is when there is passion, there are dollars beyond the norm.

Another professional fundraiser noted that the events in Israel revealed that Israel can still be

a motivator for giving. Our donors care about Israel and many new givers gave

to the Federation: 12–15 percent of the donor pool turns over each year. The total number of givers is flat, but in the 2002 campaign [we had a] net surplus of
1,000 donors. [This was the] first-time [we had] more donors [2001–02] in
eighteen years. [We also] had fewer dropouts—less than the usual 12–15 percent.

The experience of the attack in Israel on the night of the first Passover Seder, perhaps especially because this observance is so popular among American
Jews (with a large majority of them reporting attending a Seder according to all
three NJPS studies), awakened a connection between American Jews and Israel.
This connection to Israel (which a large majority of American Jews openly expressed according to all three NJPS studies) led more of them to put their money
where their mouths were and helped to explain the increase in contributions reported previously.

As one federation director noted: "Israel is still a priority despite arguments
that Israel does not mean much to American Jews." Another observed:

The linkage between 9/11 and the Israel Emergency Campaign and the Argentina [financial] collapse [and its impact on Jews there] led people to respond.
We raised $19 million for Jews in crisis [Israel and Argentina], which began as
a Victims of Terror Campaign. This money was all paid in 2002. [Our] technique was [to hold] parlor meetings and synagogue campaigns and this revita-
lized parlor meetings and synagogue campaigns.

The result of the IEC was as one professional stated, "putting Israel front
and center. . . . It is building unity in Israel at a time of need. [Now] we are talk-
ing about existential issues in a way that we wouldn't before and, to younger
people; it is the first time it is taking place."

The normative obligations for charitable giving in the Jewish community,
which were noted in earlier chapters and appeared to be weakening, were reas-
serted to a certain extent. Consider these observations by a federation director:
"This is one of the vestiges of obligatory giving and sense of communitarianism,
but there is a lot of cynicism about the system. Some new givers stepped forward, but the bulk of the money was from traditional sources." Another federation director, however, raised a nagging issue. The results of the campaign were:

On the one hand, extremely positive: a lot of money came in quickly and a fair
proportion came from new gifts. Of current givers to local annual campaigns,
less than a fifth gave to the IEC. *The real question is how many times can you
declare a crisis?* With the diminution of mass aliya [migration to Israel] in the
1990s, we need to make the case why people should give. *We need to raise
money—not collect money.*

Still the campaign revealed both a positive and a negative. The positive, as one
professional observed, was "a number of people here came forth with significant

gifts [and the] negative, a minority of Jews are upset with Israel over the settle-
ments. They equate the government with the people and won't give to Israel at
all."

The other major response to the question about the ways fundraising
changed in the wake of the Israel Emergency Campaign was that new or younger people stepped forward to contribute. Nearly half of the respondents to that
question reported an observation like the following from one federation director:
"For a lot of young people, they got a wake-up call. Peace is not there yet."
Another director put it this way: "For us, a large number of new people gave.
They were making a statement: 'Hineni!' [Here I am!] Our challenge is to trans-
form them from occasional givers to regular givers. Out of four thousand donors
to the IEC, fifteen hundred were new."

A third federation professional reported that the Campaign:

> brought some people out who had been removed. The Campaign allowed us to
> engage people whom we had not [engaged] before. We did sense new things.
> We had an open caucus and people announced their gifts. Young people could
> relate to what their parents did in 1967 and 1973. We're trying to find some
> avenues to engage them in Israel advocacy.

Another director noted the tension between the regular campaign and an
emergency fund drive, which

> created a challenge in a regular campaign. People responding to the IEC and [a]
> poor economy make the annual campaign feel ordinary. But it is vital. We
> found some new givers. How do we construct a map that includes the sum of
> annual campaigns and special campaigns. [We] need to market how an individ-
> ual feels about giving.

The hopes of many directors about the results of the Israel Emergency Campaign were summarized by one who said: "I would hope that they would capture
the new donors, but it's too early to say."

Applicability of Jewish Experience to General Fundraising

In conversation with fundraisers, especially within the context of college and
university development, about this investigation into Jewish charitable giving,
the development officers spontaneously offered unsolicited praise for the accomplishments of the national umbrella and local Jewish federation organizations. Such testimonials raise the question of "what experience, if any, of American Jewish fundraising is applicable to fundraising in general, for example, the
United Way and other charities?"

In general, there was less consensus among the twenty-five professionals interviewed on this question than on the earlier topics addressed. The most frequent responses, offered by one-fifth of respondents, dealt with the *need to build community and a sense of obligation to the community.* As one Jewish community fundraising director stated it succinctly, "The ability to raise serious money is dependent on a sense of community and common heritage."

Another executive replied: "What are we good at? We have a long history of doing it and we have a long memory. We are distinguished in this way. . . . It is not our wealth that makes us look good. There should be a moral purpose to philanthropy."

Perhaps the most telling comment was the one director who linked the success of fundraising to community-building and stated: "United Way raises money and gives it out. The federation mission is to build a Jewish community and raising money is a way to build community. There is a collective model."

Another one-fifth of respondents responded to the question of the applicability of Jewish fundraising to general charities by *emphasizing the notions of individual relationship and trust.* Thus, one federation professional observed that "to fund social services, you need to rely on an individual basis of appeal rather than a corporate appeal. To create a milieu for giving, leaders [must] give exemplary gifts." Similarly, a third executive observed:

> There is a big difference between Jewish and other forms of charities. Our philanthropy is designed to work based on personal one-on-one solicitation. United Way goes to corporations to solicit gifts through payroll deduction. . . . Most other charities do not have major gifts campaign.

Reaffirming the personal relationship in fundraising, was the theme of another federation executive: "What the Jewish community has done better than anyone else is personal solicitation." Finally, another executive summarized the implications by saying that:

> the traditional American Jewish paradigm of engaging lay leadership in meaningful roles is an expandable tool. People give to causes to which they have a personal relationship. Creating social networks has universal value. Limitations are sometimes not on the donor side but on our [Federation] side—not thinking big enough and dreaming big dreams.

Other insights observed by less than one-sixth of the professionals dealt with the *role of planned giving, the need for consistency ("relying on an anthem, theme, or mantra"), the importance of professionalism in the fundraising staff, determination of emotional concerns of donors, and reliance on peer pressure.* A postscript to this section on the applicability of Jewish fundraising experience for the general world of fundraising was the lesson offered by one executive as to what the former can learn from the latter:

Only university campaigns grow significantly because of targeted, major gifts. The university world has made significant investments in cultivating givers by learning of their interest. [Likewise,] the Jewish community needs to make investments in learning about potential donors.

Donors, Affiliated, and Unaffiliated

In Chapter Six, we examined the perceived incentives and barriers to giving as derived from our interviews with the three groups: "*Donors, Affiliated,* and *Unaffiliated*." Table 6.1 summarized the various orientations toward giving of the three groups. Since these data were gathered in the 1980s, the question arose as to whether the same incentives and barriers would be operative in the twenty-first century. Rather than gathering a new sample reflecting the three groups as noted at the beginning of this chapter, the findings from Table 6.1 were shared with the professional fundraisers to gauge the extent to which the barriers and incentives remained the same or had changed. What follows are the results of that inquiry, based on interviews with professional fundraisers who directed campaigns in communities wherein about three-quarters of American Jews lived as stated earlier.

Table 7.1 replicates Table 6.1 with the addition of the percentage of directors of fundraising who upheld as still relevant a particular category of perceived incentives or barriers. A cell that is empty had no original responses in it and, therefore, did not elicit a response from the directors. It is marked n.a. (not applicable). A cell that had an original response in it but elicited no response from the directors received a zero. The seven sets of factors which were examined to see whether they could act as incentives or barriers included: (1) Being Jewish, (2) Israel, (3) Anti-Semitism, (4) UJA image, (5) Giving Readiness, (6) Solicitation Context, and (7) Financial Situation.

In examining the six blocks of Table 7.1 including A, C, and E under incentives and B, D, and F under barriers, three of these six blocks generated the greatest responses from the directors: A, B, and F. First, Block A, tapping perceived incentives to charitable giving for the *Donors,* still demonstrated to some extent the factors promoting charitable giving to the Federations. *Among the factors most supported by one-third to two-fifths of directors was the sense of "being Jewish" (40 percent support) and "solicitation context" (32 percent). In other words, of all the incentives for giving, these two seemed to hold up the best across the span of nearly the two decades between the time the directors were interviewed and the time when the donors and non-donors were interviewed.*

Nevertheless, other Perceived Incentives in Block A still operated but were

Table 7.1 Orientations Toward Giving: Giving Valence (Perceived Incentives and Barriers to Giving) by level of Affiliation for Donors, Affiliated, and Unaffiliated, with Corresponding Percent of Support from Directors of Fundraising

	Giving Valence			
Level of Affiliation	Perceived Incentives (+)	Percent Support	Perceived Barriers (-)	Percent Support
	A		B	
Donors	(1) Being Jewish: Identifying with Jewish community, Jewish organizations, Judaism, and moral obligations (Mitzvah) of Tzedakah	40%	(1) Being Jewish	n.a.
	(2) Israel: Trips and missions build identification with Israel	25%	(2) Israel	n.a.
	(3) Anti-Semitism: Personal knowledge of Holocaust and awareness of anti-Semitism	16%	(3) Anti-Semitism	n.a.
	(4) UJA Image/Structure:	n.a.	(4) UJA Image/ Structure: Elitist, wealthy, old (no room for young leadership), catering to big givers, exploitation of federation professional, Women's Division, don't know	52%
	(5) Giving Readiness: Parent gave or relative benefits from UJA services	25%	(5) Giving Readiness	n.a.
	(6) Solicitation Context: Charismatic speaker, inspirational professional, solicitation training, informational presentation, peer-group approval	32%	(6) Solicitation Context: Public pledging, dinners, face-to-face, back-of-bus, phone, hard-sell techniques	36%
	(7) Financial Situation: Reduction in inflation	0	(7) Financial Situation: Other financial obligations (Synagogue)	25%

Table 7.1-Continued

	C		D	
Affiliated	(1) Being Jewish: Identifying with Jewish community, Jewish organizations, Judaism, and moral obligations (Mitzvah) of Tzedakah	8%	(1) Being Jewish	n.a.
	(2) Israel: Trips and missions build identification with Israel	0	(2) Israel	n.a.
	(3) Anti-Semitism: Awareness	8%	(3) Anti-Semitism	n.a.
	(4) UJA Image/Structure: Need to know, cut out administrative middle-man	12%	(4) UJA Image/ Structure: Establishment, wealthy, old, distant, invisible, not relevant, Women's Division, don't know, don't rock the boat	0
	(5) Giving Readiness	n.a.	(5) Giving Readiness	n.a
	(6) Solicitation Context: Emotional appeal, personal friend	16%	(6) Solicitation Context: Public pledging, dinners, face-to-face, phone	0
	(7) Financial Situation:	n.a.	(7) Financial Situation: No money, other financial obligations (JCC, Synagogue)	0
	E		F	
Unaffiliated	(1) Being Jewish: Moral obligation, sense of responsibility	0	(1) Being Jewish: Not interested in religious organizations, lack of Jewish identity, estrangement from religious life/Jewish culture	25%
	(2) Israel: Emergency situation or crisis, identification or concern with Israel	0	(2) Israel: Policies of Israeli government	25%
	(3) Anti-Semitism: Awareness	0	(3) Anti-Semitism	n.a.
	(4) UJA Image/Structure	n.a.	(4) UJA Image/ Structure: Lack of knowledge of the UJA, not knowing what one's contribution actually does, wealthy sponsorship	12%
	(5) Giving Readiness	n.a.	(5) Giving Readiness	n.a.
	(6) Solicitation Context: Emotional appeal, sense of duty, personal contact	0	(6) Solicitation Context: Phone calls, dinners, meetings, face-to-face, hard-sell	8%
	(7) Financial Situation	n.a.	(7) Financial Situation	n.a.

only endorsed by one-quarter to one-sixth of the fundraising directors, e.g., "Israel" (25 percent), "Giving Readiness" (25 percent), and anti-Semitism (16 percent). Given the observations noted earlier in this chapter about the decline of interest in the Holocaust and Israel (prior to the Passover attack in 2002), these findings are consistent. It should be pointed out that among these directors who cited Israel as an incentive, four of five were interviewed *after* the attack in Israel in 2002. It should be noted also, as one director observed, that Israel's economy since 1967 (the year of the Six-Day War) has multiplied much faster than the amounts donated for Israel through the Federation campaigns. In regard to item five, "Giving Readiness," its middling rank likely reflected the previously stated decline in generational continuity in giving, as noted by the directors. Finally in regard to item seven in Block A on "Financial Situation," which referred to inflation in the United States in the late 1970s and early 1980s, this was no longer an issue. Nevertheless, the previously cited testimony from the interviews with the fundraisers did show that the degree of wealth present in the Jewish community was clearly an incentive for giving.

These findings expressed by Federation directors were similar to those reported a few years earlier by Tobin, who studied trends in American Jewish philanthropy in the 1990s, based on quantitative and qualitative sources and made the following four observations:

1. Israel remains a primary motivator for giving to Jewish philanthropies. . . .
2. Building Jewish identity and community participation is a key motivator for giving. . . .
3. Social welfare and human service causes remain integral motivating forces for Jewish philanthropy.
4. Promoting social justice and fighting anti-Semitism are still salient themes for many donors (1995:2).

Turning to Block B of "Perceived Barriers" for the Donors, the most frequently cited factor by the fundraisers can be found in the "UJA [Federation] Image/Structure." More than half of directors (52 percent) cited this item, which still remained as a barrier—obviously the most salient barrier—to giving. This item was followed by "Solicitation Context" (36 percent) and "Financial Situation" of competing obligations (25 percent). Perhaps based on the proportion of responses, it is fair to say that the perceived barriers appeared to persist at a more salient level than the perceived incentives although nearly all factors still played a role in the matrix of giving. One item not picked up in Table 7.1, but alluded to in the interviews, was the recognition that despite the generosity of a sizable group of givers, many individuals in all three groups faced financial difficulties, which represented barriers to their giving. NJPS 2000–01 (United Jewish Communities 2003), using the federal poverty threshold, reported that 5 percent of American Jews were poor, drawn disproportionately from the elderly, recent immigrants, single mothers, the unemployed, and lowly educated. Even among those who were not in the federally designated poverty group, there were, according to anecdotal reports, many synagogue members or individuals involved in Jewish organizations, who were of modest means and not contributors, especially elderly widows.

In examining Block C for the "Affiliated" group, individuals who were affiliated with a synagogue or two or more organizations but did not give to the Federation, several incentives were noted. They included Solicitation Context (16 percent), followed by "UJA Image/Structure" (12 percent), "Being Jewish" (8 percent), and Anti-Semitism (8 percent). None of these factors was perceived as salient by the fundraisers as they were for the donors. In regard to Block D for the *Affiliated*, none of the items seemed to catch the attention of the directors.

Finally in regard to the "Unaffiliated" group in Block F for "Perceived Barriers," two factors, "Being Jewish" (e.g., "lack of Jewish identity, estrangement from religious life/Jewish culture") and "Israel" (e.g., the "policies of the Israeli government") caught the attention of 25 percent of the professionals as enduring barriers to giving. These items were followed by negative experiences with "UJA Image/Structure" (12 percent) and "Solicitation Context" (8 percent). In regard to Block E ("Perceived Incentives") among the "*Unaffiliated*," the directors, at least by that point at the end of the interviews, could not identify any incentives to giving.

Summary

In summarizing the evidence gathered from the interviews with the twenty-five professional fundraisers, it is reasonable to conclude that there were few contradictions among them although not all emphasized the same points to the same extent, owing to the time they were interviewed and the community in which they resided. Many of the incentives and barriers initially identified in the first phase of this research remain in place in the twenty-first century. Even some factors, which had slipped in importance, such as the role of Israel as an incentive for giving, came back into play because of the terrorism experienced there. The apparent rise of anti-Semitism in Europe and the Middle East, reported in the American press, may also restore this issue as an incentive to giving although some of these events occurred after many interviews were completed. Three of four directors who cited anti-Semitism were interviewed after the terrorist attack during the Passover holiday of 2002.

Turning more specifically to the questions posed to the professional directors, it is intriguing to compare their understanding of twenty-first-century realities as compared to the data gathered two decades earlier from the *Donors, Affi-*

liated, and *Unaffiliated*. Both positive and negative directions were examined: Among the former, the leading factors cited by two-fifths or more of respondents were the financial ability and personal desire of the donors to give, and the "entrepreneurial direction" of such giving; for the latter, about half the directors noted concern about the "quality of professionals, the mission, goals and vision, and the methods employed in the conduct of their work" along with the "competitiveness among charities—both with other Jewish as well as non-Jewish charities."

Despite these and other negative directions expressed by the directors, many saw grounds for optimism about American Jewry and its fundraising capabilities. More than two-fifths of directors noted the substantial wealth available to a significant portion of the community followed by one-third of respondents noting a strong Jewish identity among many community members. These positive assertions were counterbalanced by negative responses, most notably the "increasing assimilation of American Jews," which was observed by three-eighths of the directors.

Other questions probed the effects of terror on fundraising. Since one-half of the interviews were gathered after the terrorist attack on the United States on September 11, 2001, and the Passover attack in Israel in the spring of 2002, questions were added to the interview schedule to tap responses to these events. Little effect was observed by the post-9/11 respondents to that event. In regard to the effects of terrorism in Israel, more than three-quarters of the directors observed that Israel "re-emerged as a high priority for fundraising."

In addressing the issue of the applicability of the Jewish experience to fundraising in general, the directors showed the least consensus on this topic compared to all of the previous ones. The most frequent responses, cited by only about one-fifth of professionals, were the need "to build community" and a sense of obligation to the community as well as emphasizing the notions of individual relationships and trust.

Finally, the directors were asked to reflect on the findings from interviews with the 1) *Donors*, 2) *Affiliated*, and 3) *Unaffiliated* gathered in the 1980s in the light of the twenty-first century realities. Of the six blocks in the table summarizing incentives and barriers for the above three groups, three of the blocks stood out in generating the greatest responses from the directors. Among incentives for *Donors* (Block A), those factors which seemed to resonate most strongly across the span of two decades were "being Jewish" and "solicitation context," and they were endorsed by more than one-third of the directors. In regard to perceived barriers (Block B), more than one-half of *Donors* cited "image/structure" problems and more than one-third mentioned "solicitation context." Blocks C and D for the incentives and barriers among the *Affiliated* (non-*Donors*) produced little or no consistency of responses by the directors. On the other hand with regard to the *Unaffiliated*, the directors particularly noted that, in Block F, there were a few barriers which stood out. A total of 25 percent of the respondents noted that "being Jewish" (e.g., "lack of Jewish identity, estrangement from religious life/Jewish culture") and "Israel" (e.g., the "policies of the Israeli government") were still seen as barriers to giving. Finally, Block E, incentives for the *Unaffiliated* produced no responses.

In many ways, the changes which have occurred in the past two decades in American society and their attendant impact on the Jewish community have made the assessment of the incentives and barriers to charitable giving much more of an individualized process for each potential donor. Nevertheless, to paraphrase one of the fundraisers interviewed as to how to cut through this complexity, one might say that "*if you want to raise money from people, then find out what they are passionate about and help them fulfill their needs*" [italics for emphasis]. As one Federation fundraiser was quoted in the press as saying, "We are swimming upstream against a kind of philanthropic individualism" (Strom 2004b:F24).

Notes:

1. A special debt of gratitude is owed to Dustin Stein, graduate assistant in the Center for Judaic Studies and Contemporary Jewish Life, who helped to code the responses to the interview schedules, on which this chapter is based.

2. In most urban communities, the Federation, at the time of these interviews (2000–03), conducted one unified campaign for major Jewish charities both nationally and locally. Historically, the greatest single beneficiary of the fundraising effort was the United Jewish Appeal, which collected money on behalf of the welfare causes in Israel (as noted in Chapter Two). In New York, UJA and Federation were separate entities for a long period of time. In recent years, many federations have cut back on their allocations to Israel in favor of local groups, especially when their revenues declined in the 1990s, due to the economic recession.

Chapter Eight

Summary and Implications
for Policy and Research[1]

A medieval sage told the following story:

> Once a man was allowed to visit both Heaven and Hell. In Hell, he entered
> through an opulent palace to a luxurious dining room. There he saw a huge table
> set with a sumptuous repast. All those seated, he noted, were emaciated and had
> bulging eyes. No one ate. Since their arms were all strapped, they could not bend
> them in order to feed themselves. In Heaven, he was taken to an identical palace,
> dining room and table. Here, to his surprise, all were jovial and well fed even
> though their arms too were strapped. But since each could reach as far as his
> neighbor's mouth, everyone was able to eat. Such is the difference between
> Heaven and Hell (Kimmelman 1982:7–8).

How is "heaven" or "hell" achieved? Under what conditions do people help
each other? Not all politicians agree on a strategy as to the proper role of private
vs. public charity, and social science findings do not necessarily support the
expectations of American politicians that charity can fill the gap created by the
retreat of the federal government in providing financial support to individuals
and agencies in need.

*A variety of theoretical approaches, drawn from differing disciplines, un-
dergird research on charity:*

1. *individuals contribute because it satisfies a consumer spending need
   (economics);*
2. *individuals give because they find themselves in an immediate situation where they are constrained to do so (psychology); or*
3. *individuals donate charity out of rational self-interest (sociology and
   anthropology).*

*We propose a fourth possibility derived from social psychology: Individuals give
charity when they participate in a culture and network of social relations that
stress mutual interdependence and mutual responsibility, especially when that*

125

culture has socialized them to do so and they identify with it. This topic becomes all the more important to examine at a time in American society of enhanced prosperity and yet a diminished desire of the public sector to respond to the needs of the poor, especially children and the elderly. Note the remarks of a recent president of the Eastern Sociological Society (Ladner 1999:1):

> The shift toward stronger beliefs that many of the solutions rest within civil society where trust is placed increasingly in private markets, religious institutions, social service nonprofit organizations, and the like poses an additional challenge. How do we find ways to mobilize public support and civil society resources to alleviate the problems in the absence of a crisis?

Indeed, charitable giving as a topic for social scientific inquiry has been neglected in the literature. Not too long ago, there was only one entry under "charity" and three under "philanthropy" in the *Cumulative Index of Sociology Journals* (Lantz 1987), and only one of them was a research article and not a book review! Furthermore, there were no references to the concepts of "charity," "donation," "gift," or "philanthropy" in *The Encyclopedic Dictionary of Sociology* (Frank, *et al.* 1986). A more recent review similarly found no such references in *The Social Science Encyclopedia* (Kuper and Kuper 1996) or the *Dictionary of the Social Sciences* (Calhoun 2002) although the latter contained an entry for "exchange" (including "gift exchange").

Despite the fact that social psychology has developed a substantive area of investigation entitled "prosocial behavior," much of this research focuses on bystander intervention. When studies of charitable giving are carried out, they tend to examine the immediate context of the interpersonal relationship between the giver and the solicitor. By contrast, economic studies focus on consumer spending patterns, and sociological and anthropological studies focus on the role of the giving of gifts within specific societies. Thus psychological studies of situational determinants, economic studies of spending patterns, and sociological/anthropological studies of rational self-interest do not suggest another source for such charitable activity. Indeed, it may be rooted in a social psychological process of socialization to a cluster of beliefs, values, and norms favoring such behavior.

Summary of Findings

In Chapter One, charity and philanthropy were conceptualized as part of the literature on gift exchange in society. Such gifts have reached extraordinarily high levels in recent years: $260 billion in 2005, representing 2.1 percent of GDP, with three-quarters of that sum coming from individuals (with reported increases to $295 billion in 2006 and $307 billion in 2007). The largest beneficiaries of those charitable gifts in 2005 were religious congregations and denominations, which received $93 billion or 36 percent of total contributions. That religion should receive the largest share of such contributions is not surprising since charity is a central tenet in the major religious traditions.

Substantial research in the behavioral sciences, as noted above, suggests that individuals may donate charity as a function of consumer spending behaviors (the economic explanation), or situational constraints (the psychological approach), or self-interest (the sociological/anthropological perspective). Nevertheless, this work suggests another possibility, a social psychological conceptualization, which we reiterate: Individuals give charity when they participate in a culture and network of social relations that stress mutual interdependence and responsibility, especially when that culture has socialized them to identify with it.

Thus relying on a social psychological perspective, the primary objective of this book is to understand and explain the motivations of individuals to make charitable gifts from the perspectives of the donors and largely validated by directors of fundraising. While in Chapter One, the religious foundations of charitable giving and philanthropy were discussed, in Chapter Two, the different approaches to charity of Christianity, emphasizing *caritas* as caring compassion to help others, and Judaism, emphasizing *tzedakah* as obligatory demands to practice justice, were pointed out. Despite the prevalence of economic, psychological, and sociological/anthropological explanations for charitable giving, an examination of the Jewish case may lead to a deeper knowledge of the normative and social psychological bases for philanthropic behavior. A review of more than three decades of research revealed some interesting patterns as well as changes characterizing Jewish giving that provided the context for the current empirical investigation, which relied on three types of data sets available. They included:

1. NJPS data especially 1971 (n=5,790) and 1990 (n=2,441) and some references to 2000–01 (n=4,523);
2. non-probability sample of three groups of individuals (n=72), including *Donors*, *Affiliated*, and *Unaffiliated* with respect to the Jewish community;
3. non-probability sample of fundraising professionals (n=25), who represented communities comprising more than 75 percent of the entire American Jewish population.

These three data sources represent the strands which are woven together to form a whole cloth, addressing the central theme of this book of understanding charitable choices and explaining motivations for philanthropic donations. We began by examining in Chapter Three two relatively comparable NJPS surveys of 1971 and 1990, which provided data on the variables associated with giving to and activities in charitable funding. *Overall, age, family income, Jewish education, denominational preference, synagogue membership and attendance, more involvement in Jewish primary groups, more home religious practices, and a positive orientation toward Israel formed the set of normative factors that increased both giving to and activity in Jewish charitable fundraising. For many Jews, activity in Jewish fundraising, in its turn, led to activity in non-Jewish (general community) fundraising.* The most recent NJPS of 2000–01 supported the findings of the two previous surveys with increased Jewish charitable giving linked to age, income, institutional affiliations, and region of the country.

Some of these Jewish normative factors were also associated with giving to and activities in non-Jewish charities. Overall, more education, family income, activity in Jewish community voluntary associations, and contributions to Jewish charities had moderate impacts upon contributions to non-Jewish (general community) charities. Also, the size of Jewish communities was inversely related to giving to the UJA. Thus, the smaller the community, the higher the donations to UJA per 1,000 Jews, which testifies to the power of the web of cohesiveness more easily spun in smaller rather than larger communities (see also Rabinowitz et al. 1995). This supports our observation about the norm of social cohesion, i.e., the greater the degree of social integration, the higher the incidence of charitable giving.

That relatively small group of Jews who were not involved with their organized Jewish communities was propelled to non-Jewish (general) charity contributions by their education and family income. Finally, the second model of giving to non-Jewish charities explained only about half of the overall model variance that was explained by the first model of giving to Jewish causes.

Since large-scale surveys are constrained by the more limited range of questions permitted in a typical phone interview, the story we present is enriched by relying on in-depth interviews to supplement the findings presented in Chapter Three. In Chapter Four, the analysis of the small sample of seventy-two *Donors, Affiliated,* and *Unaffiliated* with respect to Jewish and general organizational involvement was introduced, and the findings were similar to the findings of the larger NJPS sample. In addition, the findings with respect to Jewish education and synagogue attendance followed the predicted pattern as did the variables of family life cycle and self-employment. *While the seventy-two cases did not constitute a probability sample, the relationship found between their general and Jewish background characteristics and their affiliation with UJA, or lack of it, was fairly consistent with the national picture obtained from the larger NJPS samples.*

The *Affiliated* and *Unaffiliated* may yet give in the future. As noted earlier, such well-known figures as Steven Spielberg, Bill Gates, or Warren Buffet made major charitable donations as they became more mature in years. Perhaps it takes role models at each level of giving to stimulate further philanthropy among peers and a concern with a legacy for posterity throughout the life cycle.

Given the similarities observed between the large sample survey data and the smaller in-depth interviews presented in Chapter Four, we went on to delineate in Chapter Five some of the differences in orientations that have emerged with respect to Jewish charitable giving based on comparisons of the *Donors*, *Affiliated*, and *Unaffiliated*. The results of the analysis of the data obtained through the in-depth interviews were presented as three separate portraits, defining the different orientations of the respondents to Jewish charitable giving and the reasons for it. First, the *Donors* had Jewish socialization experiences rooted in the family and community involvement and/or the giving of charity and were currently enmeshed in the community through organizational involvement, synagogue membership, and/or almost an exclusive Jewish friendship network, along with more than moderate incomes. Second, the *Unaffiliated*, by contrast, consisted of individuals who had very little Jewish socialization experience in the family, community involvement, or the giving of charity. This led them to be less involved as adults in the formally organized Jewish community, to have fewer informal Jewish friendship ties or be more likely to be intermarried, even though they did not disavow their Jewish identification and had only moderate incomes. Third, the *Affiliated* (with respect to the Jewish community but not UJA) resembled the *Donors*, in that they had Jewish roots and interconnections (e.g., synagogue membership and/or organizational involvement). Like the *Unaffiliated*, however, the *Affiliated* did not give because they did not possess a positive image and personal understanding of what the UJA or the local Jewish Federation did, even though many had more than moderate incomes. In part, this may be the result of not being adequately informed, as these individuals may have been much newer to the community; or this may have been the result of crude or negative solicitation techniques; or this may have resulted from the lack of tangible needs that the UJA fulfilled for these people.

The value of examining the qualitative data to enrich our understanding about charitable giving derived from the quantitative data is best observed in Chapter Six where incentives and barriers to giving were analyzed for the three groups. It was noted that the *Unaffiliated* shared with the *Donors* and *Affiliated* similar concerns about the barriers they perceived to their contributing to UJA with respect to its image or structure and solicitation techniques. Where the *Unaffiliated* differed significantly from the *Donors* and *Affiliated* was in the barrier posed by their lower level of Jewish identification. In respect to incentives for giving, they perceived that certain Jewish concerns might arouse their consciousness toward charitable giving, such as Israel or anti-Semitism. Without further cultivation of their sense of Jewishness, these charitable gifts might only be forthcoming from some in an emergency situation. *Thus, the evidence suggested that the norm of social cohesion applied more strongly to those individuals (Donors and, to a lesser extent, Affiliated) who had a stronger personal identity as a community member than those who had a weaker personal identity (Unaffiliated).*

In order to complete our assessment of charitable choices focusing on American Jews, which began chronologically with quantitative data from the 1970s–1990s (supplemented by more recent twenty-first-century sources in Chapter Three), and expanded by findings from our qualitative data, collected in the 1980s (cited in Chapters Four, Five, and Six), we offered in Chapter Seven the evidence gathered from in-depth interviews with twenty-five professional fundraisers. It is reasonable to conclude that there were few contradictions among them, although not all emphasized the same points to the same extent owing to the time they were interviewed and the community in which they resided. *Many of the incentives and barriers identified in the first phase of this research remained in place in the twenty-first century. Even some factors which had slipped in importance, such as the role of Israel as an incentive for giving, came back into play due to the terrorism experienced there. The apparent rise of anti-Semitism in Europe and the Middle East, reported in the American press, may also have restored this issue as an incentive to giving, although many of these events occurred after about half of the interviews were completed.* Three of four directors who cited anti-Semitism were interviewed after the terrorist attack in Israel on Passover in 2002.

In turning more specifically to the questions posed to the professional directors of fundraising, there was an interest in understanding the twenty-first-century realities as compared to the data gathered two decades earlier with the *Donors, Affiliated, and Unaffiliated.* Both positive and negative directions were examined: Among the positive, the leading factors cited by two-fifths or more of respondents were the financial ability and personal desire of individuals to give, and the "entrepreneurial direction" of such giving; for the negative, about half the directors noted concerns about the "quality of professionals, the mission, goals and vision, and the methods employed in the conduct of their work," along with the "competitiveness among charities—both with other Jewish as well as non-Jewish charities."

Despite these and other negative directions expressed by the directors, many saw grounds for optimism about American Jewry and its fundraising capabilities. More than two-fifths of directors noted the substantial wealth available to a significant portion of the community, followed by one-third of respondents noting a strong Jewish identity among many community members. These positive assertions were counterbalanced by negative responses, most notably the "increasing assimilation of American Jews," which was observed by three-eighths of the directors.

In addressing the issue of the applicability of the Jewish experience to fundraising in general, the directors showed the least consensus on this topic, compared to all of the previous ones. The most frequent responses cited by only about one-fifth of professionals was the need "to build community" and a sense of obligation to the community, as well as emphasizing the notions of individual relationships and trust.

Finally, the directors were asked to reflect on the findings from interviews with the 1) *Donors*, 2) *Affiliated*, and 3) *Unaffiliated* gathered in the 1980s in light of twenty-first-century realities. Of the six blocks or categories summarizing incentives and barriers for the above three groups, three of them stood out in generating the greatest responses from the directors: perceived incentives for *Donors* (Block A), perceived barriers for *Donors* (Block B), as well as perceived barriers for the *Unaffiliated* (Block F). Among incentives for *Donors* (Block A), those factors which seemed to resonate most strongly across the span of two decades were "being Jewish" and "solicitation context," and they were endorsed by more than one-third of the directors. In regard to perceived barriers (Block B), more than one-half cited "image/structure" problems and more than one-third mentioned "solicitation context." (Blocks C and D for the *Affiliated* [non-donors'] incentives and barriers produced little or no consistency of responses by the directors.) On the other hand with regard to the *Unaffiliated*, the directors particularly noted that, in Block F, there were a few barriers which stood out. A total of 25 percent of the respondents noted that "being Jewish" (e.g., "lack of Jewish identity, estrangement from religious life/Jewish culture," and "Israel" (e.g., the "policies of the Israeli government") were still seen as barriers to giving. (Finally, Block E, incentives for the *Unaffiliated*, produced no responses.)

In many ways, the changes which have occurred in the past two decades in American society and their attendant impact on the Jewish community have made the assessment of the perceived incentives and barriers to charitable giving much more of an individualized process for each potential donor. This suggests that the success of fundraisers may be tied to their ability to help the donors fulfill their needs about which they feel passionately.

Practical Implications for Fundraising: Micro-level Strategies

While this book is written by two sociologists and not market researchers nor organization and management consultants, the findings still suggest a series of general strategies that can be the basis for the evaluation of specific tactics to maximize the opportunities for more charitable gifts. The exact details can better be worked out by the professionals in the field in the variety of charitable endeavors which exist. The implications of the findings may be divided into two categories: the micro-level and the macro-level.

At the *macro-level*, the strategies suggested are the ones that apply to the *community* at large, and at the *micro-level*, they apply to *individuals* living in their respective localities. The former need to be addressed at the national level and the latter at the local level. *Failure to address both more or less in tandem will weaken the chances for success at either level.* This is consistent with the sociological notion that a treatment to induce planned social change is effective in proportion to its size. The bigger the treatment, the bigger the effect. This is so because there is likely to be a multiplier effect as the effects of the bigger treatment trickle down (not to be confused with "trickle down economics") to ever-increasing social layers or groups in a community. In the sections below, each of the specific strategies is indicated by a number in parentheses and concrete examples are indicated by a letter in parentheses.

The analysis of the data suggests the need for a four-fold approach at the micro-level of reaching individuals in their local communities, called the *NESS* Program, from the Hebrew word meaning miracle. (If one can put all the pieces together and be successful, one will have achieved a miracle!?) These are the four elements, which grow out of research in the Jewish community but may be equally appropriate in other sectors of society as well:

1. Name—Identification,
2. Evaluation,
3. Socialization, and
4. Solicitation.

Notice that solicitation is at the end of the process. It is not a step to be embarked upon in a casual manner.

1. The first element is *name—identification*: A substantial number of people, such as those among the *Unaffiliated* group, are not in the network and so may never be contacted to participate in the community. Therefore, *it is necessary to identify as many prospects as possible*. In this regard, specific techniques already exist, such as, identification strategies: a) *using distinctive ethno-religious names,* b) *purchasing targeted mailing lists,* as well as c) *word-of-mouth approaches*. Of course with increased population exchange through intermarriage, this strategy poses some challenges.

2. The second step is *evaluation*: a) It is necessary to *evaluate carefully each prospect* in terms of specific characteristics, such as family financial situation, perceptions of the charitable organization, and appropriate solicitation context. For Jewish philanthropy, synagogue or Jewish affiliations as well as responsiveness to Israel, anti-Semitism and the Holocaust are useful. b) The findings suggest that *there is no one right solicitation approach*; as in the business world, *segmentation of the market is very important*. Relying on computer programs, it would be possible to collect such evaluative information on new prospects and store it until an adequate portrait of characteristics is obtained.

3. The third element is *socialization* of the prospect, i.e., educating the donor. *One cannot expect people to make a commitment unless they have been led through a process of socialization experiences in support of the philanthropic purposes of the charity.* As the findings in the Jewish community suggest, giving comes out of a certain matrix of being Jewish that involves a socialization process that leads to affiliation and identification. Federations have intuitively, if not empirically, known this for awhile. That is why they have been successful and should continue to encourage *"crash courses" in Jewish socialization,* such as: a) *missions to Israel and distressed Jewish communities,* b) *adult Jewish education courses,* and c) *retreat weekends.* Another simple and relatively inexpensive way to attract the *Unaffiliated* and *Underaffiliated* would be to d) *offer a "premium"* (as public television does), such as a magazine subscription that keeps coming into the home on a regular basis. Such a premium could be made available to families who pledge an initial minimum, which is above the cost of the gift.

4. The fourth step is *solicitation. Only after all of the above steps have been implemented should solicitation be undertaken.* Only then does it have "chance for success." Here again it is important to a) *emphasize the necessity of diverse approaches for solicitation* as suggested by the findings. No one approach may work particularly well with the non-donor groups. Nevertheless, the findings suggest that some approaches that have traditionally worked well with the Donors would be spectacularly unsuccessful, such as public-pledging and card-calling. In addition, some careful consideration needs to be given in the Jewish community to the b) *creation of special local funds* that might be attractive to the *Affiliated* or *Unaffiliated* non-donors, such as educational projects or humanitarian concerns regionally or abroad. These efforts might be encouraged and expanded to include direct American aid to social and educational activities. All of this suggests the need to reconsider the possibility of permitting *new-givers* at least c) *to designate a portion of their funds* as is the practice in several general community charity drives. Finally, in regard to the Jewish community, each local Federation should be encouraged to d) *set up a Community Development Outreach Department, wherein the emphasis should be reaching out to the non-donors, who represent nationally more than half of the community.* Of course, such a program requires the allocation of professional and support staff to these activities. Without this investment in such a program, there can be no return primarily of people to the community and no return secondarily of dollars to the campaign.

Implications: Macro-level Strategies

At about the same time that the above suggested strategies are being implemented locally the following need to be undertaken nationally:

1. *An effort needs to be made at the national level to reach out to the non-donors. In the case of the organized Jewish community, the national umbrella organization (United Jewish Communities) might work in concert with other national organizations* and any other interested umbrella groups to develop a broad-based effort that would benefit all of the local constituents of these agencies: synagogues, schools, federations, and other communal agencies. In this regard, the fundraising techniques of colleges and universities in reaching out to donors ought to be emulated.

2. Every large-scale organization needs to maintain its own R and D, Research and Development, to continue to grow and adapt to changes. No less so is the case of the organized Jewish community. While much valuable basic research has been undertaken on such subjects as the Jewish family, education, identity, and anti-Semitism, not much research has been applied to the study of the *Unaffiliated*. Therefore, a first specific step at the national level would be to *initiate an academic conference on the subject of the Unaffiliated*. Research findings could be presented by those who have studied the issue and a set of policy recommendations established for appropriate agencies, such as federations, synagogues, schools, and centers. The emphasis would be on cooperation among these agencies, not competition. In the long run, encouraging individuals to make a contribution to the local federation increases the probability of their formally joining the community, and encouraging them to join a synagogue increases the probability that they will make a pledge.

3. A third step at the macro-level would be to *embark on a national campaign to identify every household in the community where potential donors might reside*. In the Jewish community, it might be called "Project Pakod," from the Hebrew word which means to *count* and also to *remember*. The objective would be simple and yet monumental: to *identify every potential Jewish family* in a given locality utilizing all of the techniques available from examining telephone books to birth announcements to contacting real estate agents. A latent benefit might be to facilitate a highly representative national Jewish population survey for the next NJPS.

4. Finally, another macro-level strategy, more applicable to the Jewish community, would be to *develop a national Jewish fund for extending*

the scope and increasing the quality of Jewish education (both formal and informal) that would bolster the transformation of Jewish education as the number one communal priority. The role of Jewish education in shaping Jewish identification has already been well documented (see Dashefsky and Lebson 2002). Several efforts along this line have already emerged, but perhaps a pool of funds could be created through the sale of bonds, which would then be used to lend or grant money to families to help pay for Jewish education.

Empirical and Theoretical Implications

While this book has had a particular substantive focus on the Jewish community, it has been informed by the larger issue of charitable giving and philanthropy in the social science literature. Therefore, these concluding observations are divided into those empirical and theoretical implications applicable to fundraising in particular in the Jewish community, as well as those relevant to the general fundraising community.

The three NJPS surveys conducted over a period of thirty years, together with numerous local Jewish community studies, clearly indicate several major social trends that must be taken into account in fundraising. First of all, the number of Jews who are involved with their organized Jewish communities will likely be undergoing a steady, slow decrease. The American Jewish birthrate is producing a relatively stable population with no increase. Indeed perhaps, the size of the Jewish population may be declining slightly although the number of households where Jews reside is certainly increasing due to intermarriage. Despite the controversy generated by recent articles in the *American Jewish Year Book 2006* about the estimated size of the American Jewish population (ranging from 5.2 to 6.4 million), one fact is dramatically clear: The share which American Jews represent of the total population of the United States has been cut approximately in half from 3.7 percent in the 1930s to about 2 percent in the early twenty-first century. (See Sheskin and Dashefsky 2006 and Della Pergola 2006.) Even recent immigration from the Former Soviet Union, South America, and Israel did not appear to offset the proportional decline.

Thus, the American Jewish population is undergoing a population exchange with the much larger non-Jewish population of the United States, which appears to show a persistently negative balance for American Jewry. Given the declining proportions who contribute to Federation campaigns or join a synagogue, Jewish Americans who regard the Jewish community with ambivalence or indifference form a significant proportion of the American Jewish population. This all adds up to fundraising from slowly declining numbers.

The major focus of fundraising likely may become education to Jewish community involvement and synagogue life. For those involved in the web of Jewish community life, the well-developed fundraising methods currently employed will continue to work. However, for those Jews more weakly involved with their Jewish communities, more subtle fundraising techniques must be developed. Such methods will concentrate on raising Jewish education levels and Jewish organizational involvement. After such programs and activities are reasonably successful, fundraising can be utilized.

The set of NJPS surveys consistently showed that a solid majority of Orthodox Jews, a majority of Conservative denomination Jews, and a solid minority of Reform preferring Jews are customarily synagogue members (see Lazerwitz, Winter, Dashefsky, and Tabory 1998). The web of Jewish involvement is based upon a foundation of synagogue memberships. Hence, the fundraising organizations must work in partnership with the synagogues. Also, as pointed out in the preceding paragraphs, such synagogue-Jewish federation partnerships will facilitate expanded information on local Jewish communities, better lists of Jewish households, and greater encouragement of participation in community research projects.

Eloquent testimony to conceptualizing the motivation for charitable gifts was offered by a prominent philanthropist:

> I base my philanthropy on a single overarching principle: that Jewish renaissance cannot be premised on a withdrawal from society or on yesterday's preoccupations with fear and victimhood. Freedom has been good to the Jewish people. We therefore must find ways to intertwine a vibrant Jewish culture with life in an open, democratic society. Making Judaism competitive with American secular culture, however difficult, is the great challenge of our day. For the non-Orthodox, we must revisit our religious practices because, for most of us, our present religious observance simply does not provide sufficient spiritual rewards. Non-Orthodox Jews must come to recognize the tremendous power of Jewish education. We must convince young Jews that their community welcomes not only their dollars but also their ideas and leadership. One way to reverse course is to base Jewish identity overwhelmingly on positive aspects of the Jewish experience—the connection to one's people, the emphasis on history and culture, and the wonders of Jewish joy (Steinhardt 2005:17).

Nevertheless, while fundraising in the Jewish community may be more successful among those involved in synagogues and Jewish organizations, attention must also be paid to the majority who do not belong to a synagogue and the one-quarter of American Jews who consider themselves "Just Jewish" (Ament 2005:11).

Does all of this make one optimistic or pessimistic about fundraising in the Jewish community? Consider the observation of Yoav Ben-Horin who explained the American Jewish fundraising scene to a British group:

> . . . in today's philanthropic climate, an increasing trend among major donors in America is accountability: the desire to know where their money is going and

how efficiently it is being spent. Philanthropists have become more assertive, demanding transparency and control. As a consequence, donations increasingly come with strings attached. This has resulted in a paradox: On the one hand, American Jewry is more organized and effective than ever in raising funds, while on the other hand it is less centralized and less given to accepting authority. This also plays itself out when it comes to choosing between giving to Jewish or to general charities. Ben-Horin explained that most American Jewish philanthropic dollars no longer go to Jewish causes, but to causes such as the San Diego Zoo or the Museum of Modern Art. This trend is even more pronounced among the younger generation, who "save whales, not Jews," he said. Despite these developments, American Jewry has not become less generous in recent years. . . . Since the start of the second Intifada, however, there has been a resurgence of concern for the state of Israel. . . . Despite his upbeat assessment, Yoav Ben-Horin warned that American donors are prone to a philanthropic "attention deficit disorder;" when they suddenly change interests and acquire new enthusiasms, this has a negative impact on charities which require consistent and stable support. On the other hand, he noted optimistically that the ever increasing numbers of young Jews now attending Jewish day schools and summer camps will eventually become generous supporters of Jewish causes in thirty years' time (*JPR News* 2004:2).

As Plotinsky (1995) observed, Jewish philanthropic tradition has been nurtured and transmitted through holiday observances, life cycle events and everyday life, and one answer to Jewish philanthropic "continuity" may be found in religious tradition. It also leads to two general observations. The first is that it is possible for a philanthropic tradition to be transmitted deliberately and systematically from generation to generation. The second is that even in a culture in which there is an extensive body of narrative literature, philanthropic behavior is learned by doing (1995:129). Remember the experience of Bernie Marcus (the philanthropic cofounder of Home Depot) and what he learned from his mother about tzedakah (as reported in Chapter Five).

By now, it is clear that fundraising successes are achieved by building upon local community networks. People will give more generously when approached through such networks. The key is to discover the strands of such networks and to employ sophisticated, socially sensitive methods of approaching people for funds.

The research presented here, and the model for giving developed from this research, considerably overlaps with the published research by Schervish and Havens (1997), which also dealt with the relationship between social participation and giving. These two researchers examined data from a 1992 survey on the topics of giving money and volunteering conducted by the Gallup Organization. They worked with a combination of cluster analysis and multiple regression statistical techniques. In their conclusions, they found that community participation variables were closely related to participation in institutions and organizations that maintain formal channels for receiving charitable contributions

(Schervish and Havens 1997:252). As they noted, "To understand giving behavior in the total population, it turns out one should focus on understanding the
community of participation, with special emphasis on the role of religious participation" (Schervish and Havens 1997:256).

Their conclusions echo the current research findings that participation in the
organized Jewish community is the key to Jewish giving and support our asser-
tion on the "norm of social cohesion:" The more people feel integrated into and
identify with a particular community or subcommunity, the more likely they are
to aid members or causes of their community or subcommunity perceived as in
need of charitable contributions. Together, their findings and those reported in
this book can readily be applied to both the American Jewish community and
the entire American population. *Therefore, in order to expand the ability of the
private sector to augment the role of government in relieving social problems, it
is necessary to improve the involvement of people in their local community networks. Furthermore, it is likely that government policies that ensure a progres-
sive fairness are more likely to engender broader citizen support.*

Conclusion

A specter is haunting American society and the European community. It is the
specter of devolution—the devolution of the responsibility for the poor, the ill,
and the infirm from the government to the citizenry. This book examines under
what conditions charity may fill the gap.

It does so by focusing on a social psychological conception of charitable
giving and philanthropic behavior as complementing the economic explanations
based on spending behaviors, psychological approaches based on situational
constraints, and sociological/anthropological approaches based on a rational
self-interest. The data utilized are drawn from one particular religio-ethnic group
that is popularly perceived and characterized as philanthropically generous,
American Jews, for which abundant data across time were available.

In summarizing the current state of American Jewish philanthropy, Wertheimer (1997) offered a balance sheet of trends, with which most Federation
directors would likely agree. On the plus side, Wertheimer observed that American Jews were noted for the following:

1. great wealth and generosity;
2. slow decline in annual federated campaign [which is] offset by gifts to
   endowment and other philanthropic foundations;
3. resilient strength of overseas Jewish donations but with more contributions going directly to the charity and not through an umbrella organization; and an

4. impressive amount of religious giving to synagogues, day schools and religious camps, among others (1997:81).

On the negative side, Wertheimer observed the:

1. shrinking base of Jewish donors, leading [fewer] people to do more;
2. changing demographics of American Jewry leading to [fewer] givers; and
3. growing sense of individualism pulling people away from communal norms of giving (1997:81–82).

Nevertheless, Wertheimer concluded that since so much of contemporary philanthropy is devoted to improving the civic life of all rather than lessening the poverty of some, "there is reason to believe that for the foreseeable future, enough Jews will heed the call to participate in and enhance the quality of Jewish life—for themselves and for all Jews" (1997:83).

With regard to the general community of fundraising, let it be noted that the retreat of government from its traditional responsibilities toward the less fortunate only exacerbates the situation. It is a reversal of a historic trend that coincides with the collapse of feudalism. The most likely effective policies in the contemporary period for alleviating social problems can come from a partnership of an engaged public sector of government institutions supported by a generous private sector of charitable organizations. Can the community afford to do less?

Note:
1. Parts of this chapter were adapted and expanded from Dashefsky and Lazerwitz (1983).

Postscript

In the aftermath of Hurricane Katrina in the late summer of 2005, as well as both the tsunami of December 2004 and the catastrophe of September 11, 2001, we were moved by the outpouring of charitable gifts by private citizens and corporate donors as well as by the volunteerism of individuals and philanthropic organizations, even as many decried the seeming ineffectiveness of various governmental authorities. Perhaps these diverse responses were the result of the sheer magnitude of the disaster spawned by the ferocity of the storm, or perhaps they were emblematic of the trend which emerged in the late twentieth and early twenty-first centuries of the devolution of responsibility from the public to the private sector for the continued need for charity. Whatever the case may be, these events highlight the need for ongoing research on the topic of charitable giving and philanthropic behavior—the subject of this book.

Despite the transformations to which we have alluded in the apparent retreat of the public sector for the application of charity, we take heart from the actions of many individuals, like one of our granddaughters who operated a lemonade stand to raise money for the assistance to victims of Hurricane Katrina. Such an action testifies to the understanding that the provision of charity is an expression of love and the pursuit of justice which aid in the repair of the world for its inhabitants. As we stated in the Preface, support for such a goal is to affirm the toast: "To Life."

Bibliography

AAFRC Trust for Philanthropy. 2002. *Giving USA 2002*. Indianapolis: The Center on Philanthropy.

———. 2005. *Giving USA 2005*. Indianapolis: The Center on Philanthropy.

———. 2006. *Giving USA 2006*. Indianapolis: The Center on Philanthropy.

Ament, Jonathon. 2005. *American Jewish Religious Denominations* (Report 10). New York: United Jewish Communities.

Andrews, Frank. 1986. *Multivariate Nominal Scale Analysis*. Ann Arbor: Institute for Social Research, University of Michigan.

Andrews, Frank, and Robert Messenger. 1973. *Multivariate Nominal Scale Analysis*. Ann Arbor: Institute for Social Research, University of Michigan.

Andrews, Frank, James Morgan, and John Sonquist. 1969. *Multiple Classification Analysis*. Ann Arbor: Institute for Social Research, University of Michigan.

Benson, P. L., and V. Catt. 1978. "Soliciting Charity Contributions—Parlance of Asking for Money." *Journal of Applied Social Psychology* 8(1): 84–95.

Berkowitz, L., and W. H. Connor. 1966. "Success, Failure and Social Responsibility." *Journal of Personality and Social Psychology* 4: 664–69.

Blalock, Hubert. 1969. *Theory Construction: From Verbal to Mathematical Formulation*. Englewood Cliffs, NJ: Princeton University Press.

———. 1979. *Social Statistics* (2nd rev. ed.). New York: McGraw-Hill.

Boskin, Michael J., and Martin Feldstein. 1977. "Effect of the Charitable Deduction in Contributions by Low-Income and Middle-Income Households: Evidence from International Survey of Philanthropy." *Review of Economics and Statistics* 3 (August): 351–54.

Calhoun, Craig, ed. 2002. *Dictionary of the Social Sciences*. New York: Oxford University Press.

Chaves, Mark, and Sharon L. Miller (eds.). 2002. *Financing American Religion*. Walnut Creek, CA: Altamira.

Cheal, David. 1988. *The Gift Economy*. New York: Routledge.

Chiswick, Barry R. 1991. "An Economic Analysis of Philanthropy." Pp. 3–15 in Barry A. Kosmin and Paul Ritterband (eds.), *Contemporary Jewish Philanthropy in America*. Savage, MD: Rowman & Littlefield Publishers.

Cohen, Steven M. 1979. "Trends in Jewish Philanthropy." *American Jewish Year Book* 80: 29–51.

———. 2004. *Philanthropic Giving Among American Jews: Contributions to Federations Jewish and Non-Jewish Causes* (Report 4). New York: United Jewish Communities.

D'Antonio, William V., James D. Davidson, Dean R. Hoge, and Ruth A. Wallace. 1989. *American Catholic Laity in a Changing Church.* Kansas City, MO: Sheed and Ward.

Dashefsky, Arnold. 1987. "Orientations Toward Jewish Charitable Giving." Pp. 19–34 in Nahum M. Waldman (ed.), *Community and Culture: Essays in Jewish Studies.* Philadelphia: Gratz College Seth-Press.

———. 1990. "American Pluralism and the Jewish Community." Pp. 203–25 in Seymour Martin Lipset (ed.), *American Pluralism and the Jewish Community.* New Brunswick, NJ: Transaction.

Dashefsky, Arnold, and Bernard Lazerwitz. 1983. *Why Don't They Give? Determinants of Jewish Charitable Giving.* Storrs, CT: Center for Judaic Studies and Contemporary Jewish Life.

Dashefsky, Arnold, Bernard Lazerwitz, and Ephraim Tabory. 2003. "A Journey of the 'Straight Way' or the 'Roundabout Path:' Jewish Identity in the United States and Israel." Pp. 240–60 in M. Dillon (ed.), *Handbook of the Sociology of Religion.* Cambridge, UK, and New York: Cambridge University Press.

Dashefsky, Arnold, and Cory Lebson. 2002. "Does Jewish Schooling Matter? A Review of the Empirical Literature on the Relationship Between Jewish Education and Dimensions of Jewish Identity." *Contemporary Jewry* 23: 96–131.

Dashefsky, Arnold, and Howard M. Shapiro. 1974. *Ethnic Identification Among American Jews.* Lexington, MA: Lexington Books.

Della Pergola, Sergio. 2006. "World Jewish Population, 2006." *American Jewish Year Book* 106: 559–601.

Durkheim, Emile. 1933/1893. *The Division of Labor in Society* (a translation of his *De la Division du Travail Social,* with an estimate of his work by George Simpson). New York: Macmillan.

Elazar, Daniel J. 2002. "Organizational and Philanthropic Behavior of the North American Jewish Community." *Contemporary Jewry* 23: 183–94.

Everatt, David, Adam Habib, Bris Maharaj, and Annsilla Nyar. 2005. "Patterns of Giving in South Africa." *Voluntas: International Journal of Voluntary and Nonprofit Organizations* 16(3):275–91.

Feldstein, Martin, and Amy Taylor. 1976. "The Income Tax and Charitable Contributions." *Econometrics* (November): 44(6): 1201–22.

Ferris, James M., and J. Michael Woolley. "Gifts of Time and Money." Unpublished article in *1991 Working Papers.*

Fishman, Sylvia Barack. 2001. *Jewish and Something Else: A Study of Mixed Married Families.* New York: American Jewish Committee.

Frank, A. W., R. Lachmann, D. W. Smith, J. V. Sorenson, R. Warner, and A. Wells. 1986. *The Encyclopedic Dictionary of Sociology,* 3rd ed. Guilford, CT: Dushkin Publishing Group.

Galaskiewicz, J. 1985. *Social Organization of an Urban Grants Economy.* Orlando, FL: Academic Press.

Gold, Steven J. 1997. "Women's Changing Place in Jewish Philanthropy." *Contemporary Jewry* 18: 60–75.

Goldberg, Jacqueline, and Barry A. Kosmin. 1998. Pp. 93–115 in *Patterns of Charitable Giving Among British Jews.* London: Institute for Jewish Policy Research.

Goldin, Milton. 1976. *Why They Give: American Jews and Their Philanthropies.* New York: Macmillan.

Goldstein, Alice. 1991. "Dimensions of Giving: Volunteer Activity and Contributions of the Jewish Women of Rhode Island." Pp. 93–115 in Barry A. Kosmin and Paul Ritterband (eds.). *Contemporary Jewish Philanthropy in America.* Savage, MD: Rowman & Littlefield Publishers.

Goren, Arthur. 1970. *New York Jews and the Quest for Community: The Kehillah Experiment, 1908–1922.* New York: Columbia University Press.

Gouldner, A. W. 1960. "The Norm of Reciprocity: A Preliminary Statement." *American Sociological Review* 25: 161–78.

Greeley, A. M., and W. McManus. 1987. *Catholic Contributions: Sociology and Policy.* Chicago: Thomas More Press.

Grossman, Cathy Lynn. 2003. "Step by Step, A Way to Give." *USA Today,* December 17: 10D.

Hall, Peter Dobkin. 1997. "Devolution: Implications for Research, Testing and Practice." Paper presented at Yale University (January 28).

Harris, M. B., S. M. Benson, and C. L. Hall. 1975. "The Effects of Confession on Altruism." *Journal of Social Psychology* 96(2): 187–92.

Harrison, Michael, and Bernard Lazerwitz. 1982. "Do Denominations Matter?" *American Journal of Sociology* 38: 356–77.

Havens, John J., and Paul G. Shervish. 2001. "The Identification Theory and the Allocation of Transfer Between Family and Philanthropic Organizations." Paper prepared for the Center for Retirement Research, Woodstock, VT (archive).

Heilman, Samuel C. 1975. "The Gift of Alms: Face to Face Giving Among Orthodox Jews." *Urban Life and Culture* 3(4): 371–95.

Hodgkinson, V. A., and M. S. Weitzman. 1986. *The Charitable Behavior of Americans.* Washington, DC: Independent Sector.

Hoffman, Shaun. 2006 "For U.S. Charities, A Crisis of Trust." MSNBC (November 21), retrieved via http://www.msnbc.msn.com/id/15753760.

Hoge, Dean R. 1994. "Introduction: The Problem of Understanding Church Giving." *Review of Religious Research* 36: 2 (December): 101–10.

Hoge, Dean R., and Douglas L. Griffin. 1992. *Research on Factors Influencing Giving to Religious Bodies.* Indianapolis: Ecumenical Center for Stewardship Studies.

Hoge, Dean R., Charlie Zech, Patrick McNamara, and Michael J. Donahue. 1996. *Money Matters.* Louisville, KY: Westminster John Knox Press.

Hoover, Dennis R. 2001. "Yes to Charitable Choice." Pp. 183–85 in Andrew Walsh (ed.), *Can Charitable Choice Work? Covering Religion's Impact on Urban Affairs and Social Services.* Hartford: The Leonard E. Greenberg Center for the Study of Religion in Public Life, Trinity College.

Hrung, Warren B. 2004. "After-Life Consumption and Charitable Giving." *The American Journal of Economics and Sociology* 63(3): 731–45.

Independent Sector. 2002. *Faith and Philanthropy: The Connection Between Charitable Behavior and Giving to Religion.* Washington, DC: Independent Sector.

Isaacs, Ron. 2005. *Kosher Living.* San Francisco: Jossey-Bass.

Jones, Keely S. 2006. "Giving and Volunteering as Distinct Forms of Civic Engagement: The Role of Community Integration and Personal Resources in Formal Helping." *Nonprofit and Voluntary Sector Quarterly* 35(2): 249–66.

JPR News. 2004. "The Interface Between Philanthropy and Policy in the United States" (Winter): 2.

Kerkman, Leah, and Cassie J. Moore. 2005. "How the Chronicle Compiled Its Annual Philanthropy 400 Rankings." *The Chronicle of Philanthropy*, October 27, retrieved via www.philanthropy.com.

Kimmelman, Reuven. 1982. *Tzedakah and Us.* New York: National Jewish Resource Center.

Kuper, Adam, and Jessica Kuper. 1996. *The Social Science Encyclopedia,* 2nd ed. New York: Routledge.

Ladner, Joyce. 1999. "Letter from the President." *Newsletter: Eastern Sociological Society* 13(2): 1, 11.

Lantz, J. C. 1987. *Cumulative Index of Sociology Journals, 1971–1985.* Washington, DC: American Sociological Association.

Lazerwitz, Bernard. 1977. "The Community Variable in Jewish Identification." *Journal for the Scientific Study of Religion* 16 (December): 361–569.

———. 1978. "An Approach to the Components and Consequences of Jewish Identification." *Contemporary Jewry* 4 (Spring/Summer): 3–8.

———. 1979. "Past and Future Trends in the Size of American Jewish Denominations." *Journal of Reform Judaism* (Summer): 77–82.

Lazerwitz, Bernard, and Michael Harrison. 1979. "American Jewish Denominations: A Social and Religious Profile." *American Sociological Review* 44 (August): 656–66.

Lazerwitz, Bernard, J. Alan Winter, Arnold Dashefsky, and Ephraim Tabory. 1998. *Jewish Choices.* Albany, NY: SUNY Press.

Leonhardt, David. 2008. "What Makes People Give?" *The New York Times Magazine,* March 9: 45–49.

Lever, Janet. 1976. "Games Children Play." *Social Problems* 23 (4): 478–87.

Lewin, Tamar. 2001. "Charity Funds Shift to West, Spreading the Wealth." *New York Times,* July 1, retrieved via www.nytimes.com.

Lord, James Gregory. 1981. "Marketing Nonprofits." *Grantsmanship News* 9 (Jan./Feb.): 53–57.

Lowenberg, F. M. 1992. "Volunteerism and Volunteering in Bible and Talmud: Implications for Contemporary Voluntary Organizations." Paper presented at the Third International Conference on Voluntary and Non-Profit Organizations, Indiana University Center on Philanthropy, Indianapolis (March).

Mauss, Marcel. 1954/1925. *The Gift.* Glencoe, IL: Free Press.

Mollenhauer, Linda. 1987. Personal letter (December 18).

Monson, Rela Geffen. 1991. "Patterns of Giving of Some Jewish Career Women: A Preliminary Investigation." Pp. 117–131 in Barry A. Kosmin and Paul Ritterband (eds.), *Contemporary Jewish Philanthropy in America.* Savage, MD: Rowman & Littlefield Publishers.

Moran, John. 1999. "Rich Ideals from Gates." *Hartford Courant*, June 17: F1,8.

Neusner, Jacob. 1982. *Tzedakah: Can Jewish Philanthropy Buy Jewish Survival?* Chappaqua, NY: Rossel Books.

Odendahl, Teresa. 1990. *Charity Begins At Home: Generosity and Self-Interest Among the Philanthropic Elite.* New York: Basic Books.

Ostrower, Francie. 1995. *Why the Wealthy Give: The Culture of Elite Philanthropy.* Princeton: Princeton University Press.

Plotinsky, Anita, H. 1995. "From Generation to Generation: Transmitting the Jewish Philanthropic Tradition." *New Directions in Philanthropic Fundraising,* Spring: 117–31.

Press, Aric. 1995. "The More We Give." *Newsweek,* September 18: 56–57.

Rabinowitz, Dayle Friedman, and Judith Tuchman Shapiro. 1981. *Among Friends: A Qualitative Analysis of Informal Jewish Friendship Networks.* Unpublished M.A. Thesis, Hebrew Union College.

Rabinowitz, Jonathan, Bernard Lazerwitz, and Israel Kim. 1995. "Changes in the Influence of Jewish Community Size and Primary Group, Religious and Jewish Communal Involvement, 1971 and 1990." *Sociology of Religion* 56(4): 417–32.

Reece, William R. 1979. "Charitable Contributions—New Evidence on Household Behavior. *American Economic Review* 69(1): 142–51.

Reingen, Peter H. 1978. "Inducing Compliance with a Donation Request." *Journal of Social Psychology* 106(2): 281–82.

Rimor, Mordechai, and Gary A. Tobin. 1991. "The Relationship Between Jewish Identity and Philanthropy." Pp. 33–56 in Barry A. Kosmin and Paul Ritterband (eds.), *Contemporary Jewish Philanthropy in America.* Savage, MD: Rowman & Littlefield Publishers.

Ritterband, Paul. 1991. "The Determinants of Jewish Charitable Giving in the Last Part of the Twentieth Century." Pp. 57–72 in Barry A. Kosmin and Paul Ritterband (eds.), *Contemporary Jewish Philanthropy in America.* Savage, MD: Rowman & Littlefield Publishers.

Ritterband, Paul, and Steven M. Cohen. 1979. "Will the Well Run Dry? The Future of Jewish Giving in America." National Jewish Conference Center, Policy Studies '79, New York (mimeo).

Ross, Aileen D. 1968. "Philanthropy." Pp. 72–80 in David L. Sills (ed.), *International Encyclopedia of the Social Sciences,* volume 12. New York: Macmillan.

Salamon, Julie. 2003. *Rambam's Ladder: A Meditation On Generosity and Why It Is Necessary To Give.* New York: Workman Publishing.

Saxon-Harrold, Susan K. E., and Jill Carter. 1987. *The Charitable Behaviour of the British People.* Tonbridge, Kent: Charities Aid Foundation.

Schervish, Paul G. 2001. "Wealth and Commonwealth: New Findings on the Trends in Wealth and Philanthropy." *Nonprofit and Voluntary Sector Quarterly* 30(1): 5–25.

Schervish, Paul G., and John J. Havens. 1997. "Social Participation and Charitable Giving: A Multivariate Analysis." *Voluntas* 8(3): 235–60.

Schoenfeld, Eugen, and Stjepan G. Meštrović. 1989. "Durkheim's Concept of Justice and its Relationship to Social Solidarity." *Sociological Analysis* 50(2): 111–27.

Schwartz, Robert A. 1970. "Personal Philanthropic Contributions." *Journal of Political Economy* 78(6): 1264–91.

Sheskin, Ira M. 2001. *How Jewish Communities Differ*. New York: North American Jewish Data Bank.

Sheskin, Ira M., and Arnold Dashefsky. 2006. "Jewish Population in the United States, 2006." *American Jewish Year Book* 106: 133–93.

———. 2007. "Jewish Population in the United States, 2007." *American Jewish Year Book* 107: 133–205.

Siegel, Danny. 1982. *Gym Shoes and Irises*. Spring Valley, NY: Townhouse Press.

Silber, Ilana F. 2000. "Beyond Purity and Danger: Gift-Giving in the Monotheistic Religions." Pp. 115–32 in Toon Vandevelde (ed.), *Gifts and Interests*. Louvain, Belgium: Peeters.

Sonquist, John, Elizabeth Baker, and James Morgan. 1971. *Searching for Structure (Alias AID III)*. Ann Arbor: Institute for Social Research, University of Michigan.

Stark, Rodney, and Roger Finke. 2000. *Acts of Faith: Explaining the Human Side of Religion*. Berkeley: University of California Press.

Steinhardt, Michael H. 2005. "Save Jews, not Harvard." *Jerusalem Post*, Feb. 11: 17.

Stirling, A. P. 1964. "Gift." P. 289 in Julius Gould and William L. Kolb (eds.), *A Dictionary of the Social Sciences*. Glencoe, IL: Free Press.

Strom, Stephanie. 2004a. "Charitable Giving Holds Steady, Report Finds." *The New York Times*, June 22: A12.

———. 2004b. "Big But Not Easy." *The New York Times*, November 15: F1, 24.

———. 2005. "Charitable Giving Outpaces that from Other Disasters." *The New York Times*, Sept. 13: A24.

———. 2006. "Billionaire Gives a Big Gift But Still Gets to Invest It." *The New York Times*, Feb. 24: A12.

———. 2008. "Increase in Charitable Giving Dampened by Signs of Belt Tightening." *The New York Times*, June 23: A14.

Sundel, H. H. 1978. "Fund-raising: Understanding Donor Motivation." *Social Work* 23(3): 233–36.

Tamari, Meir. 1987. *With All Your Possessions: Jewish Ethics and Economic Life*. New York: Free Press.

Tenenbaum, Shelly. 1993. *A Credit to Their Community*. Detroit: Wayne State University Press.

Tobin, Gary A. 1995. *American Jewish Philanthropy in the 1990s*. Research Report. Waltham, MA: Brandeis University.

———. 2004. "Jewish or Non-Jewish Philanthropy: How About Both?" *United Synagogue Review* 57(1): 31–32.

Tobin, Gary A., and Julie Lipsman. 1984. Pp. 137–66 in Steven M. Cohen, Jonathan S. Woocher, and Bruce A. Phillips (eds.), *Perspectives in Jewish Population Research*. Boulder, CO: Westview Press.

Tobin, Gary A., Jeffrey R. Solomon, and Alexander C. Karp. 2003. *Mega-Gifts in American Philanthropy: General and Jewish Giving Patterns Between 1995–2000*. San Francisco: Institute for Jewish and Community Research.

Tress, Madeleine, and Barry A. Kosmin. 1991. "Tradition and Transition in Jewish Women's Philanthropy." Pp. 75–92 in Barry A. Kosmin and Paul Ritterband (eds.),

Contemporary Jewish Philanthropy in America. Savage, MD: Rowman & Little-field Publishers.

United Jewish Communities. 1971. *National Jewish Population Survey*. New York, NY: United Jewish Communities [producer]. Storrs, CT: North American Jewish Data Bank [distributor].

———. 1990. *National Jewish Population Survey, 1990*. New York, NY: United Jewish Communities [producer]. Storrs, CT: North American Jewish Data Bank [distributor].

———. 2003. *Strength, Challenge, Diversity in the American Jewish Population: National Jewish Population Survey, 2000-01*. New York, NY: United Jewish Communities [producer]. Storrs, CT: North American Jewish Data Bank [distributor].

Van Biema, David. 1995. "Can Charity Fill the Gap? *Time*, December 4: 44–48.

Walsh, Andrew. 2001. "Introduction." Pp. 1–5 in *Can Charitable Choice Work? Covering Religion's Impact on Urban Affairs and Social Services*. Hartford: The Leonard E. Greenberg Center for the Study of Religion in Public Life, Trinity College.

Weinberger, Paul. 1972. "Conflict and Consensus Around Jewish Welfare Fund Allocations: An Interpretation." *Jewish Social Studies* 34 (October): 354–64.

Weitzman, Murray, Nadine Jalandoni, Linda Lamkin, and Thomas Pollak. 2002. *The New Nonprofit Almanac Desk Reference*. San Francisco: Jossey-Bass.

Wertheimer, Jack. 1997. "Current Trends in American Jewish Philanthropy." *American Jewish Year Book* 97: 3–92. New York: The American Jewish Committee.

Winter, J. Alan. 1985. "An Estimate of the Affordability of Living Jewishly." *Journal of Jewish Communal Service* 61(Spring): 247–56.

Woocher, Jonathan S. 1986. *Sacred Survival: The Civil Religion of American Jews*. Bloomington and Indianapolis: Indiana University Press.

Wurst, Nancy Henderson. 2003. "Giving Back." *Southwest Airlines Spirit* 12(8): 42–45.

Yinon, Yoel, and Irit Sharon. 1985. "Similarity in Religiousness of the Solicitor, the Potential Helper, and the Recipient as Determinants of Donating Behavior." *Journal of Applied Psychology* 15: 726–34.

York, Alan. 1979. *Voluntary Associations and Communal Leadership Among the Jews of the United States*. Unpublished Ph.D. dissertation, Department of Sociology, Bar-Ilan University, Ramat-Gan, Israel.

York, Alan, and Bernard Lazerwitz. 1987. "Religious Involvement as the Main Gateway to Voluntary Association Activity." *Contemporary Jewry* 8: 7–26.

Index

About the Authors

Arnold Dashefsky is professor of sociology and founding director of the Center for Judaic Studies and Contemporary Jewish Life as well as director of the Berman Institute—North American Jewish Data Bank at the University of Connecticut. He helped to found the Association for the Social Scientific Study of Jewry, along with Bernard Lazerwitz and several others, in 1970–71, serving as the first secretary-treasurer, and later as vice-president and president, as well as editor of *Contemporary Jewry*. He is the co-author or editor of six books, including *Ethnic Identification Among American Jews* with H. M. Shapiro, *Ethnic Identity in Society*, and *Americans Abroad: A Comparative Study of Emigrants from the United States* with J. DeAmicis, B. Lazerwitz, and E. Tabory, as well as the author or co-author of numerous articles and publications focusing on Jewish identity and related topics.

Bernard Lazerwitz is a professor emeritus at Bar-Ilan University in Israel. He has published over seventy-five articles, chapters, and books dealing with a variety of topics in the social sciences. His main research approach has been to use quality surveys in a study of social problems. In particular, he has studied a wide variety of issues in both the American and Israeli Jewish communities. He also was the survey statistician for the first Jewish National Jewish Population Survey (1971), which is the most precise study of the American Jewish community. In addition, he pioneered in the development of basic statistical data on the American Jewish community, covering topics such as its size, education, and socioeconomic achievements, and has explored the extent of population exchanges among the religio-ethnic groups in the United States. He is co-author of *Jewish Choices*, with J. A. Winter, A. Dashefsky, and E. Tabory.